Venture Theory

THE ART OF SCALING A BRAND

SOWMYA CJ

notionpress.com

INDIA • SINGAPORE • MALAYSIA

Contents

INTRODUCTION: The Tale Of Two Milkmen

IN STARTUPLAND, the day begins before dawn. Vendors wipe the sleep from their eyes, and the rich scent of freshly brewed coffee winds its way through narrow lanes, stirring the city awake. The morning brew, comforting and familiar, awaits one essential companion: milk. And as if on cue, two milkmen set forth with dreams as big as the steel cans they haul—Doodhwaala and Country Delight.

The clinking of bottles and the low hum of cowbells form an early-morning symphony that signals a story far bigger than mere dairy deliveries.

Doodhwaala's Dairy Dilemma

Doodhwaala dreamt of scale. Their strategy? Expand everywhere, fast. Eggs, bread, groceries—all in one app. But speed without stability is a recipe for chaos. Their logistics strained, finances leaked, and operations tottered under the weight of doing too much, too soon. Ambition, once their superpower, became their undoing.

Country Delight's Creamy Conquest

Country Delight rose with the clarity of morning light. They picked one promise—farm-fresh milk—and perfected it. Their strategy wasn't to deliver everything, but to deliver one thing with such consistency that customers remembered the taste with a smile. Trust built bottle by bottle. Their reputation spread like steam over a chai cup: quietly.

While Doodhwaala expanded wide, Country Delight dug deep.

One became a cautionary tale.

The other, a case study.

That's the heart of Venture Theory.

Country Delight didn't win by doing more, faster. They won by doing one thing well—and repeating it every single day. They built systems that scaled before they scaled the business. They turned process into culture. That quiet discipline—those small, daily improvements—are what separate startups that endure from those that explode and fade.

Venture Theory is built on that insight: that meaningful systems, decisions and strategic and timely interventions that silently compound. Like *Atomic Habits* for startups, Venture Theory argues that small, consistent actions—when embedded into an organisation's DNA—can drive seismic, long-term change.

What Lies Ahead

The next ten chapters explore strategies and real-world examples that show how focusing on small, steady improvements and habit formation can lay the foundation for a startup's success.

1. **Iterative Product Development to Counter Perfection Paralysis – The 1% Better Approach:** Why chasing perfection often holds startups back, and how making small, continuous improvements based on user feedback leads to meaningful innovation over time. This chapter also covers the importance of fostering a community around your product early on—and the risks of ignoring it.

2. **Getting the Customer Acquisition Engine Going:** Why building a vibrant user community isn't optional—it's essential. Practical ideas for how startups can actively engage customers, turn users into advocates, and create momentum that fuels sustainable growth.

3. **Growth vs Scale - Lessons from Venture Capitalists on What Truly Builds Enduring Startups:** A warning against the dangers of scaling before you're ready—with insights drawn directly from venture capitalists on what truly makes a startup worth funding. This chapter unpacks why solving for sustainable growth matters far more than chasing rapid expansion, the hidden risks of premature scaling, and what investors look for when deciding whether a company is built to last.

4. **Building a Brand, One Day at a Time:** How consistent, everyday efforts create powerful brands. It's a look at why branding isn't a one-off campaign but a daily discipline, and what happens when startups undervalue it.

5. **The Pitfalls of Ignoring Customer Experience:** Many startups falter not because their idea is bad, but because they stop listening to their customers. This chapter outlines simple steps to stay aligned with real customer needs and build a customer-centric growth engine.

6. **Solving the Non-Dilution Challenge:** Growing your company without losing your vision. This chapter tackles the tricky balance between fundraising and staying true to your mission, with tips on choosing the right investors and maintaining founder control.

7. **Storytelling vs. Substance: Why Valuations Mean Little Without Value Creation:** In the rush to raise bigger rounds and perfect pitch narratives, many founders lose sight of what matters most—solving real problems and building lasting value. This chapter unpacks the gap between perception and performance and the cost of losing sight of real value creation—and how financial discipline can anchor a startup through highs and lows.

8. **The Strategic Importance of Diversification:** Throwing more resources at problems doesn't always fix them. This chapter makes a case for being lean, scrappy, and creative—and explains how strategic diversification, not just more spending, drives resilient growth.

9. **Testing for Market Fit to Avoid the Rigidity Trap:** Markets shift. Customers evolve. This chapter emphasizes why startups must build the habit of constant market testing to avoid becoming rigid—and how a strong feedback loop can keep you flexible and relevant.

10. **The Power of 'Invisible Work'—Building Strong Foundations That Scale:** In the rush to grow, critical groundwork often gets ignored. From backend systems to process discipline and team culture, this chapter explores the often-overlooked foundations that quietly enable startups to scale without hitting painful bottlenecks later.

1.

Addressing the critical focus areas to overcome Perfection Paralysis in Product Development

CHAI  POINT

When Amuleek Singh decided to venture into the chai business, he understood the power of starting small but with a clear purpose. Instead of waiting for the perfect product, Singh embraced the Minimum Viable Product (MVP) mindset. He believed in launching quickly, gathering feedback, and iterating based on real user insights. This approach was instrumental in recognizing the untapped potential of premium-ising chai, even as the market posed challenges with price sensitivity. The result is the brand that proudly boasts the tagline "India runs on chai" – CHAI POINT.

Phase 1: The Discovery Phase

The initial phase of Chai Point's journey was a whirlwind of discovery. Amuleek, a seasoned techie, delved deep into understanding retail dynamics, consumer behaviour, and the intricacies of the product category. They learned early on about the resistance to price increases among mid to lower-tier consumers. But understood that to elevate the chai experience, the delicate balance between cost and quality had to be found. This period of intense learning highlighted the need for a premium chai experience and set the stage for Chai Point's future growth.

Reflected Amuleek Singh when he elaborated on that phase of Chai Points story

"The first discovery was the need for timely increase in price and the resistance from the consumer, which taught us how to maintain discipline around gross margins keeping in pace with inflation."

Chai Point's journey took a significant turn with a decision to pivot from targeting the mid to lower-tier market to focusing on tier 1 consumers. This decision was validated by a breakthrough partnership with Infosys, facilitated by a personal email to Mr. Narayan Murthy of Infosys Technologies. Opening a store within the Infosys Bangalore campus exposed Chai Point to their target audience who appreciated and were willing to pay for a premium chai experience. This shift not only reinforced Chai Point's premiumisation strategy It paved the way for further expansion, including securing a space at Bangalore International Airport, solidifying Chai Point's position in the market.

Phase 2: Iterative Development and Building SOPs

With a foundational understanding of the market, Chai Point moved into the next phase: creating Standard Operating Procedures (SOPs) to ensure consistency and quality. At the time, no one in India had developed SOPs for making chai at scale. Amuleek applied his engineering mindset to standardise every aspect of chai preparation—tea grade, milk to water ratio, boiling time, and more.

Chai Point's first major step in ensuring quality was the introduction of colour-coded sachets for different chai variants. Each sachet contained the exact amount of ingredients needed for one litre of chai. This innovation laid the foundation for a robust supply chain engine and facilitated consistent product quality across all stores.

This phase culminated in the creation of the **Mountain Trail Academy**, a training and certification centre. Staff were taught to replicate the same high-quality chai—whether brewing a single cup or multiple litres. The academy ensured quality didn't dilute as scale increased.

Phase 3: Automation and the Birth of Brewing Bots

As Chai Point expanded, the pressure to maintain consistency across a growing number of stores intensified. This challenge ushered in the third phase: automation. Since relying solely on manual preparation was proving to be unsustainable, particularly given the variability in LPG stove flames and the high cost of LPG.

The solution was to switch to induction stoves, which offered more consistent heating. However, this transition required solving for induction service, repair, and maintenance. The real breakthrough came with the development of cloud-connected brewing bots. These bots used LIDAR technology to ensure precise, consistent brewing of chai across all locations.

Consistency, once a goal, now became a guarantee.

Phase 4: Scaling and Market Expansion

The present phase of Chai Point's journey involved scaling and market expansion. With consistent quality assured, Chai Point was ready to reach new heights. Chai Point had deployed 6,500-7,000 brewing bots, powering all its stores and guaranteeing a consistent product experience. The focus on brewing bots not only revolutionised chai preparation but also set a new standard for the entire sector.

Chai Point's story teaches us that perfection is not a prerequisite for success. Instead, it is the willingness to learn, adapt, and innovate that truly drives growth and creates lasting impact.

We can break down this approach to building a resilient and responsive product strategy by focusing on **Six Critical Focus Areas to Overcome Perfection Paralysis**:

1. **Embrace the MVP Mindset**
   - **Focus on Launching**: Prioritize launching a Minimum Viable Product (MVP) that addresses the core problem for your target audience. This approach encourages progress over perfection, allowing you to gather invaluable user feedback early in the process.

2. **Iterative Development and Feedback Loops**
   - **Continuous Improvement**: Develop a systematic approach to iterating on your product based on user feedback. This includes setting up efficient channels for collecting feedback and mechanisms for quickly implementing changes. This cycle of feedback and improvement ensures that the product evolves in alignment with actual user needs and expectations.

3. **Data-Driven Decision Making**
   - **Lean on Analytics**: Utilize data and analytics to guide development priorities and decisions. By understanding user behaviour, engagement metrics, and feedback trends, you can make informed choices about what features or improvements to prioritize, reducing the risk of spending time on less impactful enhancements.

4. **Flexible Roadmaps**
   - **Adaptability in Planning**: While having a product roadmap is crucial, it's equally important to maintain flexibility in your plans. Be prepared to pivot or adjust your roadmap based on new learnings, market shifts, or feedback, rather than sticking rigidly to a predetermined path.

5. **Cultivating a Culture of Experimentation**
   - **Foster Innovation**: Encourage a team culture that values experimentation and is not afraid of failure. By allowing room for trial and error, you can discover innovative solutions and improvements that might not have emerged from a perfectionist approach.
6. **User-Centric Design and Development**
   - **Prioritise User Needs**: Keep the focus firmly on solving user problems and enhancing the user experience. This means sometimes setting aside the pursuit of a "perfect" feature in favour of quick, impactful changes that significantly improve user satisfaction and retention.

By concentrating on these six areas, founders can navigate the challenges of perfection paralysis, ensuring that their product development process is dynamic, user-focused, and conducive to growth and innovation. This approach not only accelerates time to market but also fosters a more resilient and responsive product strategy.

Exercise Note: Building Your Startup Strategy

As you work on your startup, use this exercise note to stay focused on building a resilient, responsive product strategy. The chart below will help you reflect on each critical area, and how you plan to apply it to your startup:

1. Embrace the MVP Mindset

What is the core problem your MVP solves?

____

____

____

Launch Date Target:

____

Key features for MVP:

____

____

____

2. Iterative Development and Feedback Loops

Feedback Channels (e.g., surveys, user interviews):

____

____

____

How often will you gather feedback?

____

____

____

Planned changes from feedback:

____

____

____

3. Data-Driven Decision Making

Key metrics to track (e.g., user engagement, churn rate):

____

____

____

Tools/Platforms for analytics (e.g., Google Analytics):

____

____

____

Decisions informed by data:

____

____

____

4. Flexible Roadmaps

Initial roadmap (3-6 months):

____

____

____

Potential adjustments based on new data or feedback:

____

____

____

How will you adapt to market shifts?

____

____

____

5. Cultivating a Culture of Experimentation

List upcoming experiments or features to test:

____

____

____

How will you ensure your team embraces failure as part of the process?

____

____

____

How often will you review results of experiments?

____

____

____

6. User-Centric Design and Development

What is the primary user problem you are solving?

____

____

____

How will you prioritize user feedback in future updates?

____

____

____

Quick wins for user satisfaction:

____

____

____

This exercise note is designed to be your quick reference and guide as you develop your product. Keep it updated and refer back to it to ensure your product development remains focused, flexible, and user-driven.

By filling in the chart as you progress, you ensure that your strategy evolves with real-time data, feedback, and market shifts.

2.

Getting the Customer Acquisition Engine Going

IN THE POST-DELTA wave of 2021, as cities slowly stirred awake from lockdowns and routines began to resume, three colleagues in Bangalore—Aman Gupta, Varun Sadana, and Vineet Khanna—placed a quiet but confident bet on an emerging opportunity to revolutionise the then nascent pet industry in India and build SUPERTAILS, a Bangalore-based startup.

It was a pivotal moment—customers had begun to trickle in, drawn by curiosity and the promise of convenience especially in the face of the still ongoing global lockdowns due to the pandemic. Yet, something felt amiss. Many would engage briefly, make a single purchase, then disappear. They quickly faced a stark realization: acquiring customers wasn't the challenge—retaining them was.

They discovered within the first few months that in the pet care industry, the stakes were different. Transactions alone wouldn't build a sustainable business; customers here sought trust, empathy, and genuine care. Pets weren't products; they were family members, deeply intertwined in their owners' lives. Thus, building trust wasn't merely beneficial; it was essential.

"Being customer-obsessed is not a poster on the wall for us—it's in the way we live every single interaction. We have zero tolerance for a bad customer experience."

A Customer-Centric Reinvention

Determined to change the course, the founders of SUPERTAILS introduced an innovative approach: Pet Relationship Managers (PRMs). Determined to shift gears, the team introduced a novel approach: **Pet Relationship Managers (PRMs)**. These weren't traditional customer service agents. They were trained pet parents, empathetic listeners, and bridge-builders.

Their brief? Engage, not upsell. After a customer's first order, a PRM would call to connect—simply asking, "What's your pet's name?" or "How old is she?" These gentle questions weren't surveys; they were stories in the making. Customers felt seen. Heard. Understood.

In a category where emotion often outweighed logic, this approach transformed Supertails from a transactional platform into a relationship-driven brand. These conversations weren't just about data collection; they forged emotional bonds. Customers began to see Supertails not as just another vendor, but as a trusted partner in their pet parenting journey.

Building Trust, One Layer at a Time

Trust, as the Founders came to learn, wasn't instantaneous. It was built layer by layer, interaction by interaction. Understanding this, Supertails began sending personalized pet ID tags free of cost—a thoughtful gesture that resonated deeply with pet parents. This wasn't a calculated marketing tactic; it was a sincere expression of care. Such small gestures reinforced the message: Supertails genuinely cared.

But they didn't stop there, they recognised that engagement went beyond just empathy—it needed to be supported by genuine expertise. Supertails began offering complimentary vet consultations, enabling customers to access professional advice easily. Although costly, they viewed it as an investment in trust. Each consultation represented a bridge of credibility between

Supertails and its customers, assuring them of the startup's unwavering commitment to their pets' well-being.

Shifting Focus: Retention Over Acquisition

With these initiatives, Supertails' focus shifted dramatically from aggressive customer acquisition to deep, relationship-based retention. This shift wasn't arbitrary; it was strategic. They knew the perils of pouring money into customer acquisition without a robust retention strategy and hence, envisioned a community-driven growth model, where satisfied customers became advocates, spreading the word organically.

This hunch paid off. As word-of-mouth spread, customer acquisition began to accelerate naturally, driven by genuine advocacy rather than costly promotions. The ripple effect was profound, reinforcing their founding belief that building a vibrant ecosystem of engaged users and advocates was far more valuable than chasing transient growth.

Creating a Culture of Empathy and Engagement

Throughout this transformation, Gupta also emphasised building a culture rooted in empathy and genuine care within Supertails. Employees weren't just trained in transactional efficiency; they were encouraged to embody the very values they promoted externally. Supertails fostered an environment where empathy wasn't just a customer-facing tactic but a fundamental internal value. This alignment between internal culture and external engagement ensured authenticity in every customer interaction.

Practical Steps and Strategic Insights

The approach had clear, practical underpinnings. First, humanising the brand became paramount. Every interaction, call, or gift reinforced the core belief that customers were valued partners, not merely revenue streams. Second, the startup doubled down on retention rather than chasing expensive, short-term growth. By creating memorable experiences, loyalty grew organically. Third, emotional connection became central, understanding deeply that the pet-parent bond is profoundly emotional.

Supertails' journey wasn't without challenges. Aman acknowledges the constant tension between short-term profitability and long-term trust-building initiatives. Yet, he remained unwavering in his belief that sustainable growth required patience and genuine care.

Looking Ahead: Sustaining Growth Through Community

Supertails continues to evolve, but the foundational principles remain unchanged. All the three founders remain deeply committed to a customer acquisition strategy that continues to be driven by empathy, trust, and authentic relationships and the belief that the organisations growth isn't measured merely by revenue or user numbers but, by the strength of its community of engaged users and passionate advocates.

Reflecting on the journey, Aman Gupta emphasised a fundamental lesson:

> *"..customer acquisition in emotional categories like pet care transcends traditional metrics. It's about nurturing a vibrant ecosystem, built on genuine relationships and mutual respect. For Supertails, this approach has proven not only effective but profoundly fulfilling."*

A Framework for Transforming Startups into Strong Brands Through Customer Acquisition and Retention

1. **Understand the Customer Acquisition vs. Retention Equation**
   - **Diagnose:** Identify whether your challenge is truly customer acquisition or retention. Most startups invest heavily in acquisition without addressing retention, leading to unsustainable growth.
   - **Prioritize Retention:** Shift focus toward deep customer engagement and retention to foster organic growth.

2. **Humanize Your Brand**
   - **Emotional Connection:** Move beyond transactions to create genuine emotional connections. Understand that customers, especially in emotional categories, seek empathy, trust, and authenticity.
   - **Personalization:** Implement personalized interactions (e.g., follow-up calls, thoughtful gestures) to transform customer interactions from transactional to relational.

3. **Implement Relationship-Centric Roles**
   - **Dedicated Relationship Managers:** Introduce specialized roles (e.g., Pet Relationship Managers) focused on customer relationships, not sales. Ensure these representatives share genuine empathy and personal experience relevant to your market.
   - **Continuous Training:** Equip relationship managers with training that emphasises empathy, listening skills, and problem-solving capabilities.

4. **Build Trust through Layered Engagement**
   - **Incremental Trust Building:** Recognize trust as cumulative, built through repeated positive interactions. Each customer touchpoint should reinforce your core values and brand promise.

- **Tangible Expressions of Care:** Provide meaningful gestures or small gifts (e.g., personalized items) that resonate emotionally, reinforcing your genuine care for the customer.

5. **Integrate Expertise into Customer Support**
   - **Offer Expert Advice:** Integrate professional expertise into customer service offerings (e.g., complimentary consultations with experts or professionals). This adds credibility and trust.
   - **Invest in Trust:** View the cost of expert engagement as a long-term investment in customer loyalty, not merely as a short-term expense.

6. **Leverage Community-Driven Growth**
   - **Advocate Creation:** Turn satisfied customers into brand advocates through exceptional experiences. Foster organic word-of-mouth as a primary acquisition channel.
   - **Community Engagement:** Build active communities around your product or service, facilitating connections between customers to strengthen collective loyalty and advocacy.

7. **Align Internal Culture with External Engagement**
   - **Culture of Empathy:** Embed empathy and customer-centric values deeply into company culture, ensuring alignment between internal operations and external interactions.
   - **Employee Empowerment:** Encourage employees to embody and practice the brand values consistently, creating authenticity in customer engagements.

8. **Measure and Optimise for Long-Term Value**
   - **Track Emotional Metrics:** Measure success not just through financial metrics but also through emotional metrics such as customer satisfaction, trust levels, and advocacy rates.

- **Continuous Improvement:** Regularly review and refine engagement strategies based on feedback and performance metrics to maintain relevance and effectiveness.

Transforming a startup into a strong brand with a robust customer acquisition engine requires a fundamental shift in approach—from short-term, transaction-focused growth to long-term, relationship-driven engagement. By prioritising empathy, trust-building, and community-centric strategies, founders can create sustainable growth fuelled by passionate advocates and deeply loyal customers.

3.

Solving for the Growth vs Scale Dilemma

Securing Venture Capital: A Blueprint for Startup Success

WHEN FOUNDERS STEP into the startup arena, raising venture capital can feel like crossing a mythic threshold. But funding is not just about a pitch deck or a promising idea—it's about showing investors that you're not only solving a meaningful problem but that you're the right person to scale that solution. It demands clarity, conviction, and the capacity to endure.

Venture capital firms today do more than write cheques. They evaluate startups through a layered lens—team strength, product-market fit, traction, scalability, financial hygiene, and founder mindset. They invest not just in potential, but in resilience. They also with examining competitive landscapes, regulatory risks, and the scalability of the business model.

By providing strategic guidance and leveraging their industry networks, VCs not only fund startups but also help them secure future rounds, build sustainable revenue models, and position themselves for long-term success.

While each venture capital firm brings its own philosophy, investment thesis, and operating model, the common thread is clear: disciplined capital deployment anchored in conviction.

This chapter distills insights from three leading VC firms—3one4 Capital, BeyondSeed Ventures, and Verlinvest (V3)—

to provide a nuanced guide for first-time founders seeking funding.

Drawing from in-depth interviews and founder-facing experience, the insights highlight not just what these firms fund, but why. By understanding their perspectives on founder qualities, market readiness, scalability, and resilience, early-stage entrepreneurs can reverse-engineer what excellence looks like at the seed and Series A stages—and refine their approach to be investor-ready from day one.

3one4 Capital: Contrarian bets rooted in clarity and conviction

3one4 Capital is known for backing companies that many other firms initially deem too early, too unscalable, or too complex. Their thesis centers around identifying underappreciated opportunities with the potential for massive long-term value. In the words of Founding Partner Pranav Pai, the firm emphasises a high signal-to-noise ratio and looks for "deep insight, not instant perfection." This is reflected in investments like Rozana.in, an agri-supply platform targeting markets that were traditionally overlooked. The firm prizes resilience and the ability to execute with precision over a flashy pitch. Rather than over-indexing on short-term profitability, 3one4 seeks founders who demonstrate obsession with the problem and a willingness to iterate fast and fail forward. Their model actively supports portfolio companies with operational infrastructure, and they are unafraid to lead when conviction is high—even in unconventional sectors.

BeyondSeed Ventures: De-risked capital with embedded operational support

BeyondSeed Ventures, led by Kuldeep Mirani, operates at the intersection of funding and functional enablement. Their model is built on "smart capital"—a combination of early-stage funding, subject matter expertise, and shared governance. Unlike traditional funds, BeyondSeed does not charge investors fees, nor do they invest in pre-revenue companies. Startups must demonstrate at least $250,000 in revenue and a dollar of profit to be considered. Their philosophy? Back businesses, not just ideas. By offering functional services like fractional CMOs, distribution support, and legal compliance via sister entities like Beyond Services and Beyond Capital, the firm significantly reduces startup failure risks. Founders must be coachable, grounded in reality, and committed to building sustainable—not just scalable—businesses. BeyondSeed's unique blend of sweat equity and milestone-linked advisory ensures skin in the game from both sides.

Verlinvest (V3 by Arjun Vaidya): Scalable consumer brands with founder-market fit

With its global roots and India-focused vision - V3 fund led by Arjun Vaidya, Verlinvest backs early-stage consumer businesses poised for breakout scale. Their thesis hinges on three key elements: exceptional founders (50% of the decision), large market potential (20%), and sound business economics and teams (30%). Vaidya brings a founder-first lens to investing, shaped by his own journey building and exiting Dr. Vaidya's. The fund specializes in brand-led ventures that go beyond D2C fads, such as Salad Days, Go Zero, and Hosteller. While the firm values financial hygiene, it is willing to work with founders through operational inefficiencies—provided there is clarity of thought and a differentiated consumer insight. Verlinvest acts not just as a capital provider, but also a brand-builder and distribution enabler, staying actively involved through structured monthly check-ins and on-demand operational support.

Backing the Bold: Inside 3one4 Capital's Framework for Venture-Scale Investing

In India's fast-evolving startup ecosystem, where capital is abundant but conviction is rare, 3one4 Capital stands out by investing in clarity over consensus. The Bengaluru-based venture capital firm has built its thesis on identifying overlooked markets, backing resilient founders, and betting early on technologies that shape tomorrow's economy. From sectors considered too nascent to markets once dismissed as unviable, 3one4's approach is defined by its structured yet contrarian lens on venture-scale outcomes.

This section explores the critical factors that influence investment decisions, offering a structured approach to help startups navigate the funding landscape effectively through the lens of 6 critical stages:

- Identifying Investment Readiness
- The Investor's Perspective
- Market readiness
- Timely Investment for Scaling
- Pitch to Secure Funding
- Trends forecasting

Stage 1: Identifying Investment Readiness
Investment Stages

Venture capital firms such as Bangalore based 3one4 Capital specialize in early-stage investments, from seed to Series A, helping startups move from ideation to scalable businesses. With a reputation for backing disruptive innovations, 3one4 Capital has invested in companies that were initially overlooked by other VCs but proved their market potential through persistence and strategic execution. These stages include:

The startup funding journey typically progresses through several stages:
- **Seed Stage:** The earliest phase, where founders have a promising idea but minimal revenue.
- **Series A:** A phase where companies have validated market fit and are generating initial revenue.
- **Series B:** At this stage, companies aim to scale their operations to meet growing demand. Funding is used to expand teams, enhance product offerings, and increase market reach. Investors expect startups to have a proven business model and substantial user base.
- **Series C:** Companies in this round focus on scaling further, entering new markets, or developing new products. The business is often profitable or nearing profitability, and the investment is used to fuel rapid growth and expansion.
- **Series D and Beyond:** These later-stage rounds are for companies seeking additional capital to achieve specific objectives, such as preparing for an initial public offering (IPO), acquiring other businesses, or developing new products. At this point, companies are well-established with consistent revenue streams.

Throughout these stages, early investors may continue to provide capital, leveraging their initial involvement to maintain equity stakes and influence in the company's growth trajectory. This sustained support can be crucial in guiding startups to successful outcomes, including achieving unicorn status.

Stage 2: The Investor's Perspective
Evaluating Risk vs. Upside

Venture capitalists analyse businesses through a risk-versus-reward lens. While potential challenges exist in every startup, seasoned investors focus on identifying why a company is positioned for success and actively work toward amplifying that success. As Pranav Pai mentioned during the interview for this book:

> *"3one4 Capital looks beyond immediate profitability and has backed companies that were initially met with scepticism and rejection by other funds due to their ambitious goals in sectors that required deep innovation."*

Resilience and Leadership

One of the most underestimated aspects of securing funding is demonstrating resilience. Founders who can continually motivate themselves and their teams while overcoming failures stand out. 3one4 Capital has repeatedly backed founders who show unwavering commitment and adaptability, believing that a strong leadership foundation is essential for navigating the unpredictable journey of scaling a startup.

ROZANA serves as a prime example—operating in a sector that had been largely ignored by institutional investors, it focused on serving small towns and rural India, where traditional retail models were inefficient. While many viewed **Tier-2 and Tier-3 commerce** as logistically challenging and financially uncertain, 3one4 Capital saw an **underserved market with latent demand**. By leveraging deep market insights, they identified that local economies were ripe for transformation, and they supported **Rozana's model of supply chain efficiency and demand prediction**—an approach that proved highly successful.

Stage 3: Key Investment Criteria

1. **The Strength of the Founding Team**

   Investors assess the founders by asking, "Would I work for this person?" Key traits that stand out include:
   - **Self-awareness**: A deep understanding of personal strengths and limitations.
   - **Co-founder dynamics**: A strong, complementary partnership that fosters problem-solving.
   - **Vision and decisiveness**: The ability to lead with clarity and conviction.

   3one4 Capital prioritizes teams that demonstrate cohesion and a shared vision. A well-balanced founding team often signals an ability to handle adversity and execute a sustainable business model.

2. **Market Viability and Timing**

   Even a strong team cannot compensate for a market that lacks growth potential. Investors prioritize:
   - Market size and scalability
   - Competitive differentiation
   - Strategic timing—why now is the right time for this business to succeed

   For example, outdated technologies, no matter how well-built, struggle to attract investment. Founders must demonstrate their market's long-term relevance. 3one4 Capital focuses on sectors undergoing transformational change, such as AI-driven automation, fintech innovations, and consumer technology disruptions.

3. **Product and Technology Readiness**

   Regardless of sector, investors evaluate:
   - **Problem-solution fit**: Is the startup addressing a critical need?
   - **Scalability**: Can the business expand efficiently?
   - **Technology as an enabler**: Does the product offer a first-mover advantage?

3one4 Capital has funded companies that leverage emerging technologies to create defensible business models, ensuring they are not just solving today's problems but are future-proofed for growth.

4. **The Secret Insight**

   Great startups often hinge on unique insights that are not widely recognized. Investors value founders who have identified these overlooked opportunities. Examples include:

   - **Dozee**: Addressing the critical shortage of nurses through AI-powered hospital monitoring.
   - **DarwinBox**: Disrupting legacy HR management systems with a more agile, tech-driven solution.

   3one4 Capital actively seeks out startups that possess a deep domain-specific advantage—secrets about a market that others have failed to recognize but hold significant potential for disruption.

5. **Scalability and Operational Execution**

   To attract venture capital, startups must prove they can:

   - Transition from early adopters to mass adoption
   - Build processes that support rapid growth
   - Achieve profitability while scaling

   Through its investments, 3one4 Capital has played a key role in helping startups establish strong operational frameworks that allow them to scale sustainably.

Stage 4: The Role of Investors in Scaling Success

Investor Expectations

VCs provide more than capital—they bring accountability and strategic oversight. Founders must be prepared to:

- Attract top-tier talent
- Define leadership responsibilities clearly
- Balance investor input while maintaining their vision

30ne4 Capital works closely with its portfolio companies to refine their hiring strategies, optimise unit economics, and navigate key inflection points in their growth journey.

Stage 5: Pitch to Secure Funding

1. **Preparing for Investor Meetings**
   Founders must arrive prepared with:
   - Market research that validates demand
   - A well-structured business model
   - A compelling pitch emphasizing their startup's unique strengths

2. **Structuring the Cap Table**
   A well-managed cap table signals investor confidence. Excessive fragmentation in early ownership can deter institutional investors, making it crucial to maintain clarity in equity distribution.

3. **Handling Rejection and Refinement**
   Rejection is an inherent part of fundraising. The most resilient founders:
   - Iterate based on investor feedback
   - Seek investors aligned with their mission
   - Remain adaptable and persistent

Stage 6: Emerging Trends in Venture Capital

1. **Shifting Investor Preferences**
   Since 2015, funding trends have evolved:
   - Increased sector diversity beyond traditional technology
   - A stronger focus on capital efficiency
   - Higher scrutiny on founder expertise and experience

   30ne4 Capital has adapted to these shifts by backing companies that emphasise financial prudence and operational resilience.

2. **Economic Cycles and Funding Availability**
   Market conditions impact funding volumes. Founders must:
   * Adapt to shifting investor expectations
   * Prepare for valuation fluctuations
3. **The Rise of Experienced Founders**
   Investors increasingly favour founders with prior startup experience. Those who have worked in high-growth environments such as successful Unicorns or from the Big 4 consulting firms are often viewed as lower-risk investments due to their industry knowledge and execution capabilities.

Venture capital success is built on three core principles:
1. **Self-awareness:** Founders must deeply understand their leadership capabilities.
2. **Market intelligence:** They must strategically position their startup for long-term growth.
3. **Relentless execution:** They must prove their ability to scale through action, not just vision.

Founders who internalize these principles improve their chances of securing investment and building a scalable, enduring company. By focusing on investor expectations and demonstrating a clear path to success, startups can navigate the funding process with confidence and clarity.

BeyondSeed: Scaling Is the Real Startup Superpower

"Build something to scale, not to sell"
says Kuldeep Mirani – the co-Founder and CEO of Singapore based Beyond Seed Venture's primary advice to founders is deceptively simple yet profound.

Yet, when raising a company, entrepreneurs often encounter a spectrum of challenges, categorized broadly under "growth" and "scale" problems. Understanding the distinction between the two and how they impact business operations and strategy is crucial for successful expansion.

This mindset shift is critical. When it comes to building startups, the allure of rapid growth often eclipses the long game. Too many startups embark on their journey with the sole intention of creating an exit strategy. However, Kuldeep emphasises that genuine value creation stems from focusing on sustainable growth rather than a quick sell. When startups focus on scalability, they naturally attract the right kind of investors and partners, and the eventual exit or acquisition happens organically as a byproduct of a well-executed business strategy.

In this section, Kuldeep lays out a founder-first capital philosophy that challenges the conventional VC playbook. Drawing on personal experience and the BeyondSeed model, he distinguishes between the tactical pursuit of growth and the strategic discipline of scaling. This distinction isn't just academic—it's the dividing line between companies that burn out chasing valuation highs and those that build enduring, self-sustaining ecosystems.

How does a Venture Capital define Growth and Scale

Growth: The Linear Path

Growth in a business context refers to the increase in size or market presence of a company through additional resources. This could mean hiring more employees, increasing production capacity, or expanding into new markets. Growth is often linear; it requires proportional increases in resources to achieve increases in output.

Scale: The Exponential Leap

Scaling, by contrast, is the ability of a company to increase its performance or revenue significantly without a corresponding rise in costs. It's the holy grail of business expansion, allowing companies to expand their reach and profitability at an exponential rate compared to their investment.

Managing Growth and Scale

Balancing growth and scale is essential for sustainable business development. Companies often focus on growth first to capture market share and establish their brand, then shift focus towards scaling operations to improve efficiency and profitability. Here are a few strategies for managing both:

- **Strategic Planning:** Have a clear vision of where you want the company to go and how you plan to get there. This includes understanding when to focus on growth and when to prioritize scaling.
- **Invest in Technology:** Leveraging technology can help automate processes and increase operational efficiency, allowing for scaling with minimal additional costs.

- **Focus on Core Competencies:** Understand what your company does best and focus on scaling these areas to maximize efficiency and value.
- **Flexible Processes:** Develop business processes and systems that are flexible and can be easily adjusted to accommodate growth or scaling needs.

In summary, the distinction between growth and scale problems lies in their focus—growth emphasises size and market presence, while scale concentrates on efficiency and capacity. Successfully raising a company requires a careful balance between these two aspects, with strategic planning and operational flexibility being key to navigating the challenges they present.

The Challenges to solve for are hence different.
Growth Problems
Growth problems are primarily associated with increasing the company's size or market presence. This includes boosting sales, entering new markets, or expanding product lines. Growth is often measured in terms of revenue, customer base, and market share increases. Key challenges include:

- **Customer Acquisition:** Finding and retaining customers can become increasingly difficult as the company tries to grow beyond its initial market. (*covered exclusively in Chapter 7*)
- **Funding for Expansion:** Securing the necessary capital to finance growth, whether through investment, loans, or reinvesting profits, can be challenging.
- **Operational Strains:** As the company grows, its existing processes, tools, and infrastructure may become insufficient, requiring upgrades or replacements.
- **Talent Acquisition and Retention:** Attracting and keeping the right talent to support growth is a significant challenge, particularly in competitive sectors. (*covered in Chapter 10*)

Scale Problems

Scale problems, on the other hand, relate to increasing the company's capacity and capabilities without compromising efficiency or profitability. Scaling is about doing more with the same or even fewer resources. Challenges in scaling include:

- **Process Optimisation:** Streamlining operations to handle increased demand without proportional increases in costs or resources.
- **Maintaining Quality and Culture:** Ensuring that the quality of the product/service and the company culture remain intact despite rapid expansion.
- **Market Saturation:** Finding new growth avenues once the existing markets are saturated.
- **Infrastructure Elasticity:** Developing an infrastructure that can scale up or down based on demand without incurring significant costs.

The Role of Innovation in Scaling

Innovation is the engine of scaling. This section discusses how continuous innovation, both in product offerings and business models, facilitates scaling. It emphasises the importance of a culture that fosters innovation and adaptability, using case studies from tech startups that have scaled rapidly by disrupting traditional industries.

Spotify uses machine learning algorithms to power its Discover Weekly feature, which introduces users to new music tailored to their tastes every week. This feature exemplifies how Spotify scales its service by enhancing user experience through technology. By continuously analysing listening habits, Spotify not only keeps existing users engaged but also attracts new users looking for a personalized music discovery experience. This strategic use of machine learning for product enhancement is a critical factor in Spotify's growth and scale strategy.

Strategic Planning for Growth and Scale

The strategic planning process for achieving growth and scaling is multi-faceted. This section provides a framework for identifying opportunities for scale, assessing market fit, and implementing strategies that balance short-term growth with long-term scalability. It introduces analytical tools and methodologies for making data-driven decisions that align with the company's vision and market dynamics.

Amazon is a prime example of a company that has mastered the art of scaling through the strategic use of big data and analytics. Amazon leverages vast amounts of data to understand consumer behaviour, optimise its supply chain, and personalize customer experiences. One key tool in its arsenal is the recommendation engine, which analyses customer purchase history, items in their shopping cart, and what other customers have viewed or purchased. By doing so, Amazon not only increases sales but also enhances customer satisfaction and loyalty, driving exponential growth without a corresponding increase in customer acquisition costs.

Lessons from Companies That Failed to Scale

Learning from failure is just as important as celebrating success. This section reflects on companies that failed to scale, analysing the reasons behind their inability to adapt to changing market conditions or leverage technology effectively. These cautionary tales serve as valuable lessons for future leaders.

Conclusion

As businesses operate in an increasingly digital and interconnected world, the ability to differentiate between growth and scaling becomes ever more critical. This chapter has outlined the theoretical underpinnings and practical applications of these concepts, providing a solid foundation for future leaders. The key takeaway is clear: while growth is essential for survival, scaling is imperative for thriving. Aspiring business leaders must embrace innovation, strategic planning, and adaptability to unlock the exponential potential of their enterprises.

VerlInvest: Cultivating Brand India in the Global D2C Landscape

At VerlInvest - Asia, under the strategic leadership of Arjun Vaidya, the emphasis is on embracing and propagating 'Brand India' across the global Direct-to-Consumer (D2C) landscape. This approach is not just about exporting goods but exporting culture, innovation, and a unique narrative that resonates with global audiences. Vaidya's insights are particularly relevant in a time when Indian brands are exploring new frontiers and are received with growing enthusiasm worldwide.

Innovation and Product Differentiation

Innovation lies at the core of VerlInvest's investment philosophy. The firm believes that the ability to innovate—to offer something uniquely appealing yet universally relatable—is what sets a D2C brand apart. This is especially crucial in competitive markets where quality and distinctiveness determine consumer preference. Arjun Vaidya emphasises that brands that fail to deliver on these fronts risk losing not just credibility but also market relevance.

Leveraging Cultural Capital

One of VerlInvest's strategic advantages is leveraging the rich cultural heritage of India—from traditional practices like yoga and Ayurveda to modern Indian innovations in textiles and technology. This 'Cultural Leverage' allows Indian D2C brands to carve out a niche in international markets. Arjun notes that this is not merely about selling products but about offering a slice of Indian culture—a practice that has seen significant success across various sectors including wellness, beauty, and consumer goods.

Customer-Centric Approaches

Rising consumer expectations around delivery and service quality are reshaping how brands operate. Speed and efficiency are now baseline expectations, especially in key urban markets. VerlInvest prioritizes investment in brands that demonstrate excellence in logistics and customer service, ensuring that these companies can meet and exceed the fast-evolving demands of their customers.

Beyond Transactions: Building Relationships

For Arjun Vaidya and VerlInvest, the transaction is just the beginning of the customer relationship. They champion brands that create memorable customer experiences—from engaging unboxing experiences to robust loyalty programs. These efforts are crucial for driving organic growth through word-of-mouth and for cultivating long-term customer relationships, which are invaluable in the volatile world of consumer goods.

Sustainable Branding

In an era where digital marketing costs continue to soar, V3 advocates for a shift towards sustainable branding. This includes investing in content marketing, influencer collaborations, and building organic distribution networks. These strategies are not only cost-effective but also build deeper connections with consumers, fostering loyalty that transcends the occasional purchase.

From Founder to Market Leader: The Advisory Role

Drawing from his rich experience as both a founder and an investor, Arjun Vaidya provides hands-on guidance to D2C brands. This mentorship is crucial in navigating the complex challenges of scaling businesses, from refining product offerings to expanding into new markets. His focus on the founder's vision and the brand's strategic direction helps ensure that investments align with long-term market trends and consumer behaviours.

Conclusion: A Vision for the Future

Under the guidance of Arjun Vaidya, VerlInvest - Asia is setting a new standard for venture-scale investing in the D2C sector. By focusing on unique product offerings, leveraging cultural heritage, and building sustainable brand practices, VerlInvest is not just funding businesses; it's nurturing global ambassadors of Brand India. As the D2C landscape continues to evolve, the insights and strategies laid out by Vaidya will be instrumental for brands looking to make a mark both in India and on the world stage. This visionary approach not only aligns with the broader trends observed by other leading venture capital firms but also highlights a unique path to success that is woven with cultural pride and innovative excellence.

Checklist for Founders expecting to raise their first series of funding:

Compiled based on dozens of interviews and investor patterns, here's the founder-ready checklist that passed the scrutiny of India's most discerning VCs.

1. **Clear Problem-Solution Fit**
   - ✓ **Have you validated that your product solves a real and urgent problem?**

   3one4 emphasises solving fundamental, structural problems that require deep insight—not just riding trends.

2. **Founder-Market Fit**
   - ✓ **Do you have a personal or professional reason to win in this market?**

   V3 backs founders with purpose and stamina to survive down cycles, not just opportunistic ideas.

3. **Early Revenue or Traction**
   - ✓ **Can you demonstrate traction—ideally at least ₹2 crore (~ \$250K) in annual revenue?**

   BeyondSeed only backs startups post-traction, with at least \$1 of profit to show a working business model.

4. **Unique Insight or Advantage**
   - ✓ **Have you identified a "secret" or overlooked insight about the market that others have missed?**

   3one4 looks for founders with domain-specific advantages that others ignore.

5. **Team Strong and Balanced Team**
   - ✓ **Do your co-founders bring different but complementary skills?**

   Investors check how well the founding team works together and shares responsibilities.

6. **Efficient Use of Capital**
    ✓ **Can you show that you're building capital-efficiently—especially in early stages?**

    All 3 VC's look for prudent financial discipline even before profitability.

7. **Defined Use of Funds**
    ✓ **Do you have a plan for how the raised capital will accelerate product, distribution, or growth—not just sustain burn?**

    BeyondSeed: "We invest in companies that need capital to grow, not to survive."

8. **Market Size and Timing**
    ✓ **Is your market large, growing, and ready for disruption now—not someday?**

    All three investors highlight TAM (Total Addressable Market) and timing as non-negotiables.

9. **Coachable and Self-Aware Leadership**
    ✓ **Are you open to feedback, mentorship, and hands-on support?**

    BeyondSeed screens out founders who are not "teachable." Coachability is essential.

10. **Resilience Under Pressure**
    ✓ **Have you shown grit in building through uncertainty or rejection?**

    All VC's prioritise founders who bounce back and keep building through failure.

11. **Clean Cap Table and Governance Hygiene**
    ✓ **Is your equity structure founder-friendly and investor-ready?**

    Poorly structured cap tables or unclear ownership discourage institutional investors early.

12. Structured, Short, Compelling Pitch Deck

✓ **Is your deck short, sharp, and focused on the "why now," "why you," and "why this?"**

BeyondSeed emphasises that a bloated, unclear pitch deck is the fastest way to lose investor interest.

4.

Building a Brand, One Day at a Time

CARAT LANE

The Data-Driven Revolution of Indian Jewellery Retail

IN JUNE 2015, Avnish Anand found himself walking back through the doors of CaratLane, the jewellery retail startup he had left four years earlier. It was an unexpected return, marked by a sense of unfinished business.

Avnish was no stranger to CaratLane's early struggles. When he left in 2011, the company was in its infancy, with a small-scale B2C business and an even smaller B2B division. By 2015, CaratLane had grown, but many of its foundational operational issues were still present. The data was maintained in silo's, and decision-making often relied more on instinct than insight. What Anand returned to was a company that had grown, yes, but also one that needed direction—and fast.

When he returned to CaratLane in June 2015, Avnish wasn't given a title. Infact he wasn't even handed a brief. But he was trusted. That trust became the foundation on which CaratLane would redefine modern jewellery retail in India.

Unlike many brands that aim for splashy campaigns and celebrity faces, CaratLane took a different route. One that was quieter, more deliberate—but ultimately, more enduring.

This is the story of how CaratLane built its brand by questioning convention, obsessing over data, and aligning customer experience with product excellence.

Phase 1: Breaking the Mold—Discovery Through Observation

In 2015 CaratLane, had grown—structurally, financially, and in ambition. But something fundamental was missing: **data-driven decision-making**. The need quickly emerged to transform CaratLane into a brand that could compete with giants, and upon reflection emerged the need to become more scientific in their approach to growth. Almost immediately, he began digging into the data. One of his first actions was to analyse the company's promotional strategy.

The marketing team ran ads. The product team built features. But both operated in silos. There was traffic, but conversions were falling. And the usual blame game had begun.

"Everyone was doing their job, but we were still not hitting targets. So the obvious question that needed solving was—*how is that even possible?*"

This led to one of Avnish's earliest interventions—they scrapped a popular 25% discount campaign after realising that many of the products only had 10% margin. A move that led to a sweeping overhaul of the pricing strategy, aligning discounts with actual profitability.

No one had crunched the numbers. And when they did crunch the numbers, a simple spreadsheet became a wake-up call.

This phase was all about asking the right questions:
- What does a store actually do for the business?
- What is the real impact of digital marketing if conversion doesn't follow?
- And most importantly, how do both channels work *together*?

Phase 2: Data as Culture—Building Foundations for Brand Decisions

As CaratLane scaled, the need for tighter systems became apparent. Avnish began by hiring analysts—not marketers, not merchandisers, but **analysts**—with one brief: "Look at the data, tell us what's happening."

What followed was a quiet revolution.

- The company mapped store-level inventory to app-level browsing data.
- Pincodes became business units. If a pincode couldn't be fulfilled due to lockdowns or stock-outs, marketing to that pincode was paused.
- The conversion journey was re-mapped, factoring in screenshots, repeat visits, and even in-store interactions.

> *"Screenshot-taking was the strongest predictor of buying intent. We optimised our remarketing based on that one insight."*
> *- said Avnish as he recollected that memory during our interview*

This was not marketing as usual. This was brand-building through intelligence. And it showed.

CaratLane didn't just think about customers—it **watched** them, **studied** them, and most importantly, **respected** their intent.

Phase 3: Omnichannel by Design—Merging Store and Screen

One of the most transformational insights came when Avnish noticed an internal tug-of-war: the online sales team and in-store sales teams were fighting over credit for the same customer.

"A customer would talk to someone online, then walk into a store and buy. The store got the credit, but the online team did the work."

To fix this, CaratLane introduced the **Joint Closure Model**—credit was shared between both teams. The friction reduced.

Collaboration improved. But more importantly, it shifted the focus from *who closed the sale* to *how the customer wanted to buy*.

In parallel, they unlocked one of their biggest assets: **dynamic inventory**. Every store's inventory was visible to the entire ecosystem. If a ring in Pune was being viewed online by a customer in Delhi, it could be shipped overnight.

And just like that, a nationwide jewellery catalogue was born—across stores, online, and try-at-home services.

Phase 4: Personalised Experiences at Scale

With systems in place, CaratLane moved to the next level: **personalisation**. But not through creepy tracking or gimmicks—instead, through simple, purposeful innovations.

- Offers were no longer just emailed; they were housed inside the CaratLane app.
- Store staff were trained to ensure every customer downloaded the app to access their unique coupons, which meant every customer's journey could be tracked across channels.
- In-store engagement became event-driven—customers were invited to clean their jewellery, celebrate anniversaries, or explore new collections curated based on their browsing history.

> *"When we knew someone from Jayanagar had browsed five designs, we made sure the Jayanagar store called them. Local, relevant, human—that's what worked."*

It was CRM, but with heart.

Phase 5: Marketing as a Function of Trust, Not Spend

CaratLane never chased celebrity endorsements. There was no glitzy IPL ad. No mega launch with red carpets. No advertisements featuring leading silver screen actresses.

And yet, the brand became ubiquitous.

THE ANSWER:

Because the product was designed beautifully. The customer experience was obsessively refined. And the marketing only *amplified* what was already working.

> *"Our brand is built by great designs first, great customer experience second, and then marketing supports both."*

The team even discovered that 40% of their new customers came from word-of-mouth or from seeing CaratLane worn by friends and family. In fact, they turned this into a deliberate strategy by showcasing real customer videos—much like Myntra TV—on the site and app.

Phase 6: Brand Building in the Age of Pincodes and Postcodes

And then came the pandemic. A historic event that forced Caratlane to dissolve the lines between online and offline services.

With lockdowns splitting the country into red, orange, and green zones, business was now driven not by geography, but by **pincode**.

Every ad, every discount, every delivery was geo-fenced. Customers were only shown what could be fulfilled from their zone. Marketing was no longer about broad messaging—it was about **hyper-local precision**.

This gave rise to one of CaratLane's most powerful frameworks—**Catchment-Based Revenue Planning**. Each pin code had its own revenue target, store strategy, marketing budget, and inventory plan.

In Avnish's own words:

> *"There was no single campaign that built CaratLane. It was built by design, experience, and an obsession with getting better every single day."*

Caratlane's lesson is proof that in the world of modern brand building, you don't need to be loud—you just need to be *clear*.

AN ENTREPRENEUR'S Recipe card

Ingredients
→ Best quality only

- 1 cup genius idea
- 1 heaping spoon of courage
- 3 tbsp of googling 'how to start a business'
- 1 gallon of caffeine
- Pinch of Luck
- Sprinkle of good friends to keep you SANE
- Adjust with creativity
- 10 drops of PANIC mixed evenly

Optimal
It's a trap!

- 1 business mentor (recommended, if available)

(TIP: Avoid seasoning with too many opinions)

1. Preheat to 'hustle mode'. Let excitement rise. (& naivité)

2. In a large mixing bowl, combine ideas & courage & google searches & chat GPT queries. Stir well till semi-coherent.

3. Slowly fold in patience (avoid lumps of frustration)

4. Add hard work + late nights one spoonful at a time

(WARNING: may cause occasional burnout. Rest as Needed.)

5. Sprinkle creativity & PROBLEM-solving (the secret ingredients!)

6. Knead in some failure - it's part of the process - don't PANIC! Adjust accordingly. It will come together.

7. Let it rise. Keep checking & tweaking.

8. Taste test - adjust - serve hot with a side of memes & chocolate to retain sanity. (too many cons...)

me time

The Evolution of Alicia Souza's Brand—From Facebook to a Thriving Online Empire

Alicia Souza's journey as an illustrator is a vivid reflection of how passion, persistence, and adaptability shape creative brands in the modern world. From investing early when she was still based in Melbourne and heading the design team at CHUMBAK, to running one of India's most loved illustration-based lifestyle brands, Alicia's story is deeply intertwined with the evolution of social media itself—and her journey holds valuable lessons for any creative entrepreneur.

The Early Days: Facebook as a Launchpad

When Alicia Souza first started out, the landscape of social media was very different. Instagram, the now omnipresent visual platform, was barely on the scene, and Facebook was the default social medium for sharing creative work. For Alicia, Facebook was her first public gallery, a place where she would religiously post one drawing a day—a routine that would later become the backbone of her visibility and growth.

But her decision to start on Facebook wasn't backed by any grand strategy—it was driven by sheer love for illustration and a refusal to be boxed into graphic design, a field she knew she didn't want to pursue.

In Alicia's own words,

> *"If you're doing brochures, you get called to do brochures. But I wanted to be known as an illustrator, so that's what I did."*

Even when work was slow, Alicia stuck to illustrating what she loved rather than what was trending or profitable at the time.

The daily discipline of sharing her art on Facebook built more than just a portfolio—it built a community. At a time when professional illustrators were scarce in India, her consistent presence drew attention, curiosity, and eventually, commissions.

Offline Hustle: Beyond Digital Walls

Her success wasn't confined to the digital world. Back then, Alicia had to supplement her Facebook presence with real-world meetings—physically visiting clients and potential collaborators. This was long before brands and artists felt comfortable finalizing deals over emails and Zoom calls. She recalls the nervousness of discussing money—a crucial but awkward conversation for many artists. But those meetings were essential, teaching her how to advocate for her worth, and shaping her understanding of the "business side" of art.

The First Brush with Product Design

Alicia's brand took a pivotal turn when she ventured into products—a leap that was both accidental and transformative. Though she always had a deep love for stationery and products (having grown up obsessing over greeting cards and stickers), she didn't intend to commercialize her art. That changed when she partnered with a friend to create small product lines—mugs, magnets, notebooks—which sold surprisingly well.

Interestingly, Alicia was reluctant to put her name on her products initially. But with time, her name became synonymous with the brand. "People would say, 'Where can I get Alicia Souza's stuff?'" she laughs, recalling how her personal identity became inseparable from her creations.

The Birth of an Online Store

As demand grew and more people wanted access to her products, Alicia realised the need for an online store. But setting up a store brought new challenges—logistics, manufacturing, and customer service—areas far removed from the artistic process.

A friend who had a background in operations stepped in at this time and managed much of the backend—from sourcing to shipping—allowing Alicia to stay focused on drawing. Even so, Alicia remembers packing and sending products that were stored under her bed, a testament to the DIY hustle behind what looked like a seamless operation on the outside.

The online store wasn't just a shop—it became an extension of her community, where people could take home a piece of her joyful, whimsical world.

Going Viral and the Instagram Era

As Instagram grew in popularity, Alicia eventually transitioned her online presence to the new platform. She admits she was a "latecomer" to Instagram, but once there, it offered a visual-first space that suited her work perfectly.

Still, Alicia remained deliberate about how she used these platforms. She was wary of becoming an "influencer"—a label she never wanted. Despite receiving brand requests for collaborations that would require her to feature her face more prominently (because algorithmically, faces get more engagement), Alicia stayed true to her identity as an illustrator. "I don't want to be called for my face; I want to be called for my work," she emphasised.

The Calendar Breakthrough and Product Expansion

Every brand has a product that changes the game. For Alicia that breakout product was her **"Grateful Calendar"**, a daily colouring calendar that combined her love for products, illustration, and positive living. The idea, conceived during a shower (which she terms her thinking sanctuary), captured the imagination of her audience. It wasn't just a calendar—it was a tool for gratitude and creativity, reflecting her personal philosophy.

The calendar's success pushed the store to new heights, and with that came a realisation—if she was to continue focusing on what she loved (illustrating), she couldn't be responsible for handling the operations side of the business.

The Strategic Partnership: Future Wagon

Enter **Saurabh Sharma**, her business partner who she met serendipitously when he sent her cat-shaped candles from his factory. Their meeting turned into a business partnership, giving birth to a professional structure behind Alicia's brand. Together, they agreed that Sourabh would manage the business side, including logistics and manufacturing, while Alicia would remain solely focused on illustration.

The company was formalised under the name **Happy Wagon**, a separate entity from Alicia personally, but exclusively producing her branded products. Interestingly, Alicia operates on a **royalty model**, meaning she earns from the sales of her products but isn't involved in day-to-day operations—a setup that allows her complete creative freedom.

Maintaining Creative Autonomy and Community

Alicia's business choices reflect a conscious effort to **preserve her creativity**. She refuses to take on projects or commitments that compromise her time for drawing. Even when asked about hiring interns or expanding operations, she prefers keeping things small and manageable to avoid diluting her craft.

What makes Alicia unique is her **deep relationship with her community**. While many brands chase numbers, Alicia focuses on **authentic engagement**. Her social media isn't just about marketing products—it's a way to share her life, thoughts, and art with her followers, making them feel part of her journey.

Her **Instagram stories, candid updates,** and reflections on motherhood and life resonate deeply, building not just a customer base but a **loyal tribe**.

Refusing to Follow Every Trend

As trends in digital marketing shift rapidly, Alicia remains selective about what she engages with. Even as brands push for more influencer-like content, she resists being boxed into formats that don't align with her identity. This clarity—knowing what to say no to—is a significant part of why her brand feels **authentic and enduring**.

Looking Ahead: Growth on Her Own Terms

Despite the pressures of growth, Alicia refuses to sacrifice her creative integrity. She prefers **slow, organic growth over scaling too fast**. "I know I could make a lot more money if I ran my own company full time," she says candidly, "but I really just want to draw."

Her story is a reminder that **success doesn't have to look like scaling endlessly**—it can look like creating joyfully, connecting meaningfully, and growing sustainably.

Today, Alicia Souza's brand stands as **one of the most beloved creative brands in India,** not just because of her art, but because of her unwavering commitment to **authenticity, creativity, and community**.

A Strategic Guideline for Startup Marketing

For early-stage startups, marketing is often viewed as a function activated post-product readiness. However, insights from CaratLane's brand evolution and Alicia Souza's organic growth journey demonstrate that marketing must be designed as a growth lever—not a postscript.

1. **Anchor the Brand in Authenticity**

   Both CaratLane and Alicia Souza built differentiated brands by first identifying their "why." CaratLane focused on democratizing jewellery shopping, while Alicia's brand expressed warmth, relatability, and personal storytelling. Startups must begin by defining their core narrative—what they stand for and why it matters. This narrative becomes the filter for all downstream decisions: from tone of voice to design elements to community engagement.

   Recommendation: Develop a brand identity matrix that includes purpose, voice, tone, visual aesthetic, and customer archetype. This acts as the north star for consistency.

2. **Segment Spend into Performance and Brand Buckets**

   Startups often overspend on performance marketing without first establishing brand recall. CaratLane invested in both: direct response ads for acquisition and brand-building initiatives for long-term trust. Alicia Souza, on the other hand, grew her brand through consistent content and community, proving that high CAC (Customer Acquisition Cost) isn't the only path to scale.

   Guideline Budget Split:

   - **50% Performance Marketing:** Paid search, social ads, retargeting
   - **30% Brand Building:** Influencer partnerships, storytelling campaigns, UGC
   - **20% Experiments/Organic:** SEO, email, events, content marketing

This 50:30:20 allocation balances measurable short-term ROI with sustainable long-term visibility.

3. **Invest Early in SEO and Owned Channels**

   CaratLane's web architecture and category pages were designed to capture high-intent search traffic—a move that reduced dependency on paid spends over time. Alicia's blog and email newsletter created repeat engagement. Startups should begin content creation and SEO optimisation in Month 1, not Month 12.

   Quick Wins:
   - Launch a blog with 3–5 pillar articles tied to high-intent keywords
   - Build an SEO-friendly site structure (collections, FAQs, reviews)
   - Initiate a lead capture strategy (newsletter or early access list)

4. **Track LTV, Not Just CAC**

   One common mistake is measuring performance marketing only by immediate conversions. Instead, startups should track **Customer Lifetime Value (LTV)** to CAC ratio. CaratLane built loyalty via cross-sells and gifting; Alicia retained customers via limited drops and storytelling. This increased payback periods and made marketing investments more defensible.

   Best Practice: Use cohort analysis and retention tracking from Day 1. Tools like Mixpanel, Google Analytics, or HubSpot help surface key metrics.

5. **Measure, Iterate, Compound**

   What differentiates successful brands is iteration. Campaigns are not "set and forget." Test copy, creative, targeting, and channels weekly. Alicia experimented with product formats and community features. CaratLane launched regional campaigns and optimised based on ROAS (Return on Ad Spend) and engagement.

KPI Dashboard Must-Haves:
- CAC by channel
- ROAS
- LTV/CAC ratio
- Organic vs Paid traffic
- Retention by cohort

The Rise of Narrative-Led Brands in a Creator-First Economy
If there's one thing that ties the journeys of CaratLane and Alicia Souza together, it's this: both brands were built on trust, consistency, and clarity of voice. They didn't chase trends. They didn't rely on celebrity endorsements. Instead, they listened to their audience, solved for intent, and focused on building systems that could scale *trust*, not just *transactions*.

In many ways, their journeys anticipated what we now see unfolding at scale across India—the rise of individual creators turning into full-fledged entrepreneurs. Over the past few years, we've seen fashion bloggers turn into apparel founders, tech reviewers launch hardware accessories, parenting content creators build early-learning brands, and wellness influencers create product lines rooted in their own routines.

These creators-turned-founders didn't begin with a business plan—they began with storytelling. Their audience came first. Products came later. What differentiated them was not just their following, but the feedback loop they built with their communities—one that guided design, pricing, positioning, and even packaging.

Today, this model of *audience-first product development* is no longer the exception—it's fast becoming the playbook. In the backdrop of a March 2025 consulting survey that revealed **over 40% of Indian teenagers aged 16–18 are considering "influencer" as a full-time career**, these shifts are more than just cultural—they're structural.

What we are witnessing is a new class of founders who don't see storytelling and entrepreneurship as separate skill sets. For them, content is not marketing—it's *infrastructure*. Trust is not a consequence—it's the *currency*. And brand is not built in boardrooms—it's built in comment sections, DMs, and late-night brainstorming sessions with their community.

As we look ahead, the question is no longer *"What product are you selling?"*

It's *"What trust have you earned—and how are you designing your business around it?"*

5.

Placing the Customer Front and Centre

Licious

Abhay Hanjura and Vivek Gupta didn't simply aim to launch a meat and seafood brand. They set out to mend a fundamental fracture in India's meat market: a lack of trust. From the earliest sketch of their idea, they understood that India's vast population of meat eaters was often forced to rely on uneven standards of hygiene and freshness. They called their venture **Licious**, and they designed it with a firm sense of purpose. Instead of treating it as an online delivery service, they built a full-stack brand that promised unmatched reliability, freshness, and convenience. They took control of the entire supply-chain, knowing that genuine trust demanded a consistent, uncompromising approach.

Today, Licious has become more than a household name. It's a benchmark for an industry that once felt chaotic, inconsistent, and marred by mistrust.

Phase 1: The Discovery—Understanding the Trust Deficit

Early on, Abhay and Vivek identified the real hurdle. It wasn't about simply offering superior meat; it was about solving a deficit in confidence. The traditional market was a puzzle of dirty conditions and unpredictable quality. They found a population large enough to sustain a thriving meat and seafood industry, yet few options existed for consumers who wanted assurance in every purchase.

They dived headfirst into research, visiting butcher shops, coastal fisheries, and poultry farms. They watched how people chose their cuts and spoke with potential suppliers. Patterns emerged: there was no dependable brand that could promise quality, safety, and convenience in one place.

That realization sparked an ambitious ambition: why not create a meat and seafood brand as reliable as a top-tier hotel's kitchen? The only way forward involved owning every link in the supply-chain.

Phase 2: Building the Foundation: Managing the Entire Supply-Chain

Once the problem was identified, it was time to bring the solution to life. The biggest challenge was ensuring consistent quality in a category where freshness is non-negotiable. Few products are as perishable as raw meat. Even a small dip in temperature could undo days of effort.

Abhay and Vivek made a sweeping decision. Licious wouldn't operate as a simple marketplace. It would manage every step from sourcing to delivery.

- **Backward Integration:** Licious constructed its own processing hubs, subjecting each cut to rigorous hygiene checks.
- **Cold Chain Infrastructure:** They introduced a continuous cold chain, holding the temperature between 0–4°C from the moment an item was sourced until the moment it arrived at a customer's doorstep.
- **No Intermediaries:** In place of the usual network of middlemen, they sourced meat directly from farms, maintaining full authority over each phase.

Though this approach demanded extensive operational heft, it defined the very promise that Licious would "never compromise on quality."

Phase 3: Creating SOPs for a Category Lacking Standards

Just like Chai Point streamlined how chai is made, Licious had to set fresh guidelines for an industry that never really had any. It was all about consistency—something that really matters to customers who worry about where their food comes from.

- **Cut Standardization**: They noticed that meat was trimmed and sliced differently across various regions. To offer uniform portions, the team set specific rules on angles, thickness, and portion size.
- **Quality Grading**: Using custom categories for freshness, marbling, and tenderness, they elevated a product that most consumers had never seen graded before.
- **Process Automation**: Machinery and technology replaced guesswork wherever possible, resulting in a product whose attributes customers could count on.

These new workflows represented a critical step toward a scalable model that repeated quality each time someone placed an order.

Phase 4: Changing Consumer Behaviour and Earning Trust

Though Licious refined its back-end operations, many consumers still held onto old habits. People liked seeing and choosing cuts in-person. An online brand that offered sealed, ready-to-cook packages had a steep hill to climb in convincing a sceptical audience.

They tackled that problem through:

- **Consumer Education:** Licious used blog posts, social media, and other content channels to explain the advantages of safely sourced, hygienically processed meat. They clarified the differences between chilled and frozen, dispelling myths that had long existed.

- **Speed and Convenience:** A 120-minute delivery promise brought Licious closer to the immediate responsiveness of the local butcher, blending digital ease with real-world quickness.
- **Uncompromising Quality:** Each item shipped with a "100% Freshness Guarantee." If a customer remained unconvinced, the order was replaced—no friction, no blame.

This trifecta of education, convenience, and unwavering standards proved to be a powerful catalyst for building trust.

Phase 5: Scaling Customer Acquisition and Creating a Community

With strong momentum, Licious looked toward scaling. It wasn't just about adding new customers. It involved turning first-time buyers into consistent supporters.

- **Subscription Model:** A recurring delivery system kept people restocking favorite items and maintained a predictable revenue flow for the company.
- **Personalisation:** AI-driven recommendations gave people suggestions aligned with dietary preferences or past orders, fostering a sense that Licious understood their unique tastes.
- **Community Building:** Social media channels and brand storytelling brought meat lovers together, celebrating the ease and satisfaction of preparing at home with reliable ingredients.

This phase involved a transformation from fledgling startup to name brand, with a reputation for hygiene and taste.

Phase 6: Reinforcing Leadership—Omnichannel Expansion
With its online operation thriving, Licious took a major step in 2024 by acquiring Bengaluru-based My Chicken and More. This signalled a deeper move into physical retail, allowing more direct contact with buyers who still favored an in-store experience.

They turned to technology wherever possible:
- **AI-Powered Demand Forecasting:** Predictive analytics helped to minimise inventory waste and shore up delivery logistics.
- **Cold Chain Automation:** They implemented real-time temperature checks so each product would stay in pristine condition.
- **Retail Expansion:** Dedicated Licious stores began reaching broader audiences.

From day one, Abhay and Vivek anchored Licious with an unwavering insistence on superb quality and a focus on how each customer felt about their purchase. They didn't simply create another company. They restructured an entire industry, erasing years of mistrust and inconvenience. By managing the supply-chain, defining industry-first standards, harnessing technology, and safeguarding consumer trust, Licious has reshaped the landscape of meat and seafood in India.

Even as they move into fresh geographies and products, their core principle remains the same: never break faith with the consumer, and never compromise the quality that defines a Licious meal.

Rethinking Quality in a Purpose-Driven Landscape: MELTED by Paper Plumes

In a world increasingly drawn to thoughtful consumption, "quality standardization" can't just be about hitting uniform targets. It needs to adopt a more flexible set of rules, supporting both integrity and innovation. **MELTED by Paper Plumes** demonstrates this fresh perspective—small in scale but rigorous in practice.

As legacy brands reimagine what "premium" will mean in the coming decade, it may be the smaller, handmade, and deliberate labels leading the way. We're already seeing packaging, label design, and brand messaging shift toward deeper intentionality. After all, luxury isn't strictly how something looks—it's also about how it makes you feel.

Every aspect of a MELTED candle—from the materials used to the packaging—tells a story. Now, the brand wants those stories to occupy centre stage.

> *"People need to understand why something is sustainable," says founder **Sana Bhatia**. "They should know what sets it apart, where it's sourced from, and who's involved in creating it."*

Yet, there's a balancing act: how does a small, artisan brand preserve its human touch while meeting the high expectations of a premium market? And more intriguingly, what can larger organisations learn from this approach?

Rethinking Consistency in a Handmade World

Traditional quality-control models—lean manufacturing, automated systems, factory-level standards—are often built for mass-scale production. For artisan producers like MELTED, a different approach is required. Sana Bhatia advocates for a "humanised" form of consistency—one that protects product integrity without erasing the brand's artisanal DNA.

MELTED's candles use plant-based waxes and essential oils sourced from various regions across India. They're hand-poured, meaning no two batches are machine-calibrated. Despite this, the company achieves over 95% consistency in both appearance and scent, thanks to meticulous documentation and hands-on training. The small variance—perhaps a shift in colour or texture—becomes a hallmark of authenticity rather than a flaw.

This method underscores a broader shift: consistency isn't about flawless uniformity anymore, but rather about delivering a reliably delightful experience. If customers expect both quality and uniqueness, the product must provide exactly that—expertly crafted, even if not identical every single time.

Rethinking Quality in a Purpose-Led Landscape

In today's market, a remarkable product alone no longer suffices. Customers expect consistency, purpose, and a commitment to sustainability—especially from artisanal or small-batch ventures. This creates a delicate puzzle: how do you preserve the appeal of handmade goods while meeting the exacting standards of a premium brand?

Conventional quality-control frameworks revolve around large-scale, automated methods that don't often fit the uniqueness of handcrafted or sustainability-focused brands. A fresh perspective is required—one that reimagines standardization to align with mindful design, ethical sourcing, and a personal touch rather than mass production.

Quality Without Absolute Uniformity

For many makers, total uniformity isn't the goal; consistent experience is. Products may show slight variations in look or feel, but quality, usability, and emotional resonance should stay constant.

Achieving this means changing how you think about standardization: it's not about erasing every difference. It's about ensuring that any variations still match the brand's promise.

Start by clarifying your brand's definition of consistency:
- **Scent Strength** for wellness items?
- **Shelf Life** for organic foods?
- **Craft Integrity** for handmade pieces?

Once these parameters are set, founders can structure training sessions, draft SOPs, and embed quality checks that deliver reliable results—without sacrificing the artisanal essence of their offerings.

Sourcing with Purpose and Precision

Many up-and-coming founders adopt decentralised sourcing—partnering with small-scale farmers, independent artisans, or regional producers. This strategy adds depth and authenticity to final products but can also introduce variations that weaken consistency if poorly managed.

To maintain high standards, brands should consider:
- **Clear Ingredient Specifications**: Define the sensory, structural, and performance criteria for each component.
- **Vendor Education**: Treat suppliers as partners aligned with your mission. Encourage them to understand the brand values and quality benchmarks.

- **Micro-Batch Testing**: Test new raw materials in small quantities before full-scale production, preventing costly or time-consuming fixes later on.

By focusing on solid, relationship-oriented sourcing, quality is integrated at the ground level—rather than patched up later in the production process.

Training as a Quality Lever

In ventures that rely on manual skills, the abilities of the team become the primary factor in ensuring product consistency. This becomes even more critical during peak demand periods that often require hiring temporary or seasonal help.

Instead of relying on informal delegation or guesswork, founders should invest early in systems that expand team capabilities without depending too heavily on a few experienced individuals.

Key strategies include:

- **Simple, Visual SOPs**: Straightforward guides, especially suited for a workforce that may have limited technical training or frequent turnover.
- **Shadowing and Mentorship**: Pairing newcomers with experienced team members maintains output quality and brand consistency.
- **Task-Specific Quality Checks**: Identify checkpoints in each production phase to quickly spot and address deviations.

When quality is owned by the whole team—not just the founder—it becomes far easier to scale operations without diluting standards.

Sustainability and Quality: A Combined Priority

Brands grounded in ethical production may worry that prioritising eco-friendly measures could clash with their precision standards. However, these values can complement each other when thoughtfully woven into both design and day-to-day operations.

For instance, switching from single-use packaging to reusable or refillable formats cuts environmental impact while creating additional customer engagement opportunities. Likewise, reusing materials (like jars, containers, or fabrics) does not necessarily sacrifice presentation, provided that visual and structural guidelines are carefully established.

When embraced systematically, sustainability often sparks innovation, rather than stifling it.

Closing the Feedback Loop

Customer feedback is a frequently overlooked resource in quality management, particularly for new or growing brands. Many founders devote energy to production oversight but fail to leverage post-purchase insights to refine standards.

High-performing early-stage ventures use feedback as an operational asset by:

- Consistently gathering product reviews, returns data, and casual remarks.
- Classifying feedback by category—packaging, scent, performance, longevity, and so on.
- Applying these insights to product adjustments or updates to standard operating procedures.

Some founders even reach out directly to key customers, discovering not only ways to improve their product but also building loyalty and goodwill in the process. By integrating feedback into their quality systems—rather than relegating it to a marketing afterthought—brands can evolve quickly and stay aligned with customer expectations.

Lessons for Founders

Although ensuring consistency in a purpose-driven, product-centric brand comes with unique obstacles, it also unlocks notable advantages. By shaping a thoughtful approach to quality, founders can infuse both resilience and distinction into their ventures from day one.

- **Define Your Version of Consistency:** For artisan and ethically focused brands, standardization is less about perfect uniformity and more about reliably delivering a consistent experience.

- **Make Sourcing Part of Your Quality System:** If you rely on decentralised suppliers, establish clear, centralised standards. Go beyond purchasing—invest in education, partnership, and oversight to ensure alignment with your brand's values.

- **Treat Training Like Product Development:** Your team's skill is your production engine. Document procedures, simplify them, and then scale that know-how as early as possible.

- **Embed Sustainability into the Design Phase:** Eco-friendly measures remain consistent only if they're built into how you create and package products. Make sustainability a foundational element rather than a last-minute adjustment.

- **Use Customer Feedback as a Quality Metric:** Incorporate real-world feedback from customers into your internal QA process. Track satisfaction with the same diligence you apply to measuring production quality.

Customer Experience as a Competitive Advantage—A Founder's Playbook

In a competitive market, a great customer experience is often what sets a successful brand apart from the rest. A well-designed experience can turn a curious visitor into a loyal customer. Whether you're launching a tech platform, retail product, or niche service, building trust, engaging your audience, and shaping each step of the customer journey are key to long-term success.

Yet, many founders find themselves stuck in transactional territory, unsure how to cultivate lasting loyalty. Customer experience spans every touchpoint, from the first flicker of brand recognition to the moments that follow a purchase. If you're aiming for authentic connections, a comprehensive plan is essential.

Below is a framework that offers guidance at every level— from quelling deep-rooted trust issues to crafting personalised interactions at scale.

1. **Identify and Fix the Trust Deficit**

    Startups often operate in spaces where customers already have doubts. Before refining your user experience, address the underlying issues that block buyers from feeling secure.

    Framework for Identifying Trust Gaps

    - **Observe Customer Behaviour:** Notice when potential buyers hesitate. If returns spike or reviews repeatedly mention the same worries, there is a signal that something needs attention.

    - **Map the Customer Journey:** Look beyond the immediate sale. Consider the research phase, decision-making, post-purchase support, and opportunities to re-engage.

- **Understand Customer Concerns:** Are users sceptical about quality or frustrated by slow delivery? Do they worry about responsiveness if something goes wrong? Solutions to these sticking points build lasting confidence.

Actionable Steps for Founders

- **Offer Radical Transparency:** Reveal the origins of your materials, outline production methods, and share realistic timelines. This openness can ease suspicion.
- **Guarantee Quality and Stand Behind It:** Make refunds or exchanges simple. When buyers realize the burden of dissatisfaction isn't on them, they approach your brand with renewed interest.
- **Educate and Engage:** If your product or service challenges existing habits, use detailed guides, webinars, or social platforms to demystify your approach.

Added Insight

Consider introducing small behind-the-scenes stories. For example, if you sell handcrafted items, show images or short videos of the artisans at work. This isn't a marketing trick—it's a personal touch that invites people to understand the care behind each product.

2. **Move Beyond Transactions—Create Personalised Engagement**

Trust paves the way, yet real loyalty often emerges through unique and relevant interactions. People seek experiences tailored to them rather than a uniform approach.

Framework for Personalised Engagement

- **Data-Driven Customisation:** Use browsing patterns, purchase histories, or real-time feedback to suggest items that fit each user's style or needs. People appreciate a brand that "gets" them.

- **Build a Community, Not a Mere Customer Base:** Vibrant brands organise events, encourage user contributions, and celebrate shared passions. A sense of belonging helps individuals feel connected to your mission.
- **Reduce Friction:** Make processes swift and painless, whether it's a mobile checkout or a user-friendly site. Speed and simplicity often define today's expectations.

Actionable Steps for Founders

- **AI-Driven Personalisation:** Algorithms can detect subtle patterns in user behaviour. Pinpointing preferences—like a favorite product category or browsing time—can shape well-timed offers and suggestions.
- **Community-First Approach:** Loyalty programmes, ambassador opportunities, and exclusive perks turn casual buyers into engaged participants.
- **Optimise Post-Purchase Experience:** Clear shipment tracking and easy returns lessen stress. Proactive support—such as follow-up messages to address common questions—transforms a standard sale into an ongoing conversation.

Added Insight

If you maintain a newsletter or social channel, give customers a place to share testimonials or personal stories. This exposure can encourage others to feel part of a broader movement instead of a single transaction.

3. **Scaling Customer Experience While Preserving Authenticity**

When a startup begins to expand across new geographies or among different teams, ensuring a unified experience becomes tricky. The risk is that efficiency gains reduce personal touches.

Framework for Scaling CX Without Losing Personalisation

- **Tech-Enabled Automation:** Tools like chatbots, knowledge bases, and CRM systems can handle basic inquiries. Resources are then freed up for conversations that require empathy or nuance.
- **Standardised Support SOPs:** A clear handbook for customer service helps distributed teams act in unison. Detailed guidelines for responses, refunds, or escalations preserve a consistent tone.
- **Proactive Customer Support:** Send alerts or updates if there's a delay or a known bug. This transparency can fend off frustration before it grows.

Actionable Steps for Founders

- **Implement Predictive Customer Service:** Use AI or analytics to sense patterns. If certain issues repeat, address them before they generate widespread dissatisfaction.
- **Balance Automation and Human Support:** Bots excel at quick fixes, though complex concerns demand empathetic, human-led conversations.
- **Measure and Iterate Relentlessly:** Track key metrics (Churn Rate, Time to First Value, NPS, etc.) to see if your efforts match expectations. Adjust processes whenever you notice a dip in user satisfaction.

Added Insight

Consider a periodic internal review where customer-facing teams recount success stories or share recurring issues. This ritual keeps everyone alert to what your users experience daily, reinforcing an empathetic culture as you expand.

Customer Success Metrics

Measuring progress is crucial to maintaining a thriving customer experience. These metrics translate user satisfaction into tangible data points, guiding future improvements:

- **Churn Rate:** Tracks how often customers leave or fail to renew. A drop suggests greater alignment with user needs.
- **Time to First Value (TTFV):** Measures how quickly a newcomer grasps the product's core benefit. A shorter TTFV means people see immediate worth.
- **Adoption Rate:** Reflects how many new users integrate your product's capabilities into their routines. It's a sign of whether your onboarding process is effective.
- **Net Promoter Score (NPS):** Indicates how likely customers are to refer you to their peers. Rising NPS often correlates with strong loyalty and brand advocacy.
- **Engagement Metrics:** Session length, frequency of visits, or daily active users (DAU) can highlight how deeply people engage with what you offer.
- **Customer Support Tickets:** Declining ticket numbers, especially around early usage or setup questions, may show that your product is more intuitive.
- **Feature Utilisation:** Helps you see if customers unlock the full potential of your platform or service.

Superior customer experiences stem from a culture that values empathy as much as innovation. Building trust, boosting engagement, and personalizing journeys aren't side projects; they represent the core of how you do business. Brands that achieve this rarely depend on features alone. Instead, they cultivate relationships, respond honestly to changing demands, and continually refine how they interact with customers. That level of dedication can place a startup on the path from modest beginnings to an enduring presence, all powered by the people it serves.

6.
Mastering the Non-Dilution Challenge

How Dozee Mastered the Non-Dilution Challenge

IN A STARTUP WORLD dazzled by term sheets and valuation chatter, money can muffle the very impulse that set the company in motion. Capital is oxygen, yet it risks thinning the blood of an idea if founders trade purpose for speed. *Dozee* (the contact-free patient monitoring pioneer) offers a counterexample: growth financed without surrendering the blueprint.

In 2015 two twenty-four-year-old engineers, **Mudit Dandwate** and **Gaurav Parchani**, stood at a fork. Acceptance letters from Carnegie Mellon and ETH Zurich lay on their desks; a family medical emergency lay heavier still on Mudit's mind. Hours of undetected distress had cost a loved one dearly. The incident dulled the gleam of academic ambition and sharpened a different question: *Could technology warn us before bodies betray us?*

Both universities agreed, somewhat incredulously, to defer admission for a year. The pair diverted tuition savings into a fledgling venture they named **Dozee**. It was less a pivot than a reckoning, turning heartbreak into hardware and data into foresight.

Phase 1: Precision Before Hype

From the outset, Dozee's north star was crisp: build a system that spots silent physiological shifts and sends word before crisis strikes. Mudit, steeped in sensor engineering, and Gaurav, fluent in machine learning models, embedded early prototypes in ward corners and bedrooms, iterating in the hum of real hospitals rather than the glow of pitch-deck slides.

By 2019 the platform could not only track vitals but also statistically flag impending deterioration, gifting nurses precious lead time. The technology's unlikely proof of concept arrived courtesy of *Pi*, Mudit's teething puppy, who settled onto a sensor mat and proved that contact-less monitoring could register even a small creature's heartbeat. Pi now owns a modest slice of Dozee equity and naps beneath Gaurav's desk, a furry footnote to the company's first breakthrough.

Phase 2: Strategic Fundraising with Visionary Investors

As Dozee moved from promising startup to serious market contender, additional capital became essential. Mudit approached fundraising with precision, welcoming only those investors who valued long-term healthcare impact over short-term valuation bumps. That discipline paid off in 2020 when Dozee secured its first significant venture infusion. By year-end the company had raised about 17.7 million dollars through three rounds. Each backer arrived not merely as a financial contributor but as a strategic partner in Dozee's mission to transform patient monitoring.

Phase 3: Maintaining Founder Control and Scaling Operations

Rapid growth made it vital for the founders to retain decision-making authority, ensuring that expansion never drifted from Dozee's core purpose. The COVID-19 crisis delivered both an enormous challenge and an unexpected catalyst. Hospitals, stretched beyond capacity, urgently needed reliable remote monitoring. Dozee's technology fit that need precisely.

Being a product conceived and manufactured in India turned into a decisive advantage when global supply chains stalled. Local production let Dozee keep hardware flowing while many rivals faced shortages. Acknowledging the importance of this capability, government bodies granted emergency clearances to Dozee and its suppliers, allowing uninterrupted manufacturing.

With logistics secured, Dozee deployed its system to more than 220 hospitals, overseeing tens of thousands of beds by mid-2020. This scale up was not a scramble; it was a faithful execution of the founders' vision, demonstrating resilience and mission alignment.

Throughout this phase Mudit and his leadership team held firm control, enabling quick pivots in a turbulent healthcare environment. Their ability to act decisively confirmed the strength of Dozee's foundations and set the stage for continued growth and innovation in patient-care technology.

Phase 4: Sustaining Core Values Through Thoughtful Brand-Building

Dozee, unlike many consumer-tech outfits that roll out new hardware every quarter, concentrates on extending the life and capability of devices already in the field. This stance highlights a commitment to sustainability and keeps the technology relevant for years rather than months. Mudit noted during our conversation that new features reach the platform only after exhaustive testing and regulatory review.

One recent upgrade added sleep-apnoea detection, addressing a serious condition that often goes undiagnosed. By layering such functions onto the existing system, Dozee amplifies its clinical impact without the environmental or financial costs that come from frequent hardware replacements.

Phase 5: The 2024 Push Toward Global Expansion and Regulatory Mastery

Dozee now pursues a larger ambition: to rank among the world's foremost health-AI companies. Key steps include:

- **International Footprint:** After a successful rollout in several African nations, Dozee entered the United States with full FDA clearance, granting access to one of the most advanced healthcare markets on the planet.

- **Regulatory Excellence:** Earning FDA approval demonstrates strict adherence to safety and performance standards. To streamline the process, Dozee shifted from local advisers to U.S.-based regulatory specialists who understand the agency's expectations in detail.

- **Early Engagement:** The founders used the FDA's pre-submission programme to gather initial feedback, allowing them to refine documentation in line with agency guidance. This foresight strengthened the final application.

- **Efficient Navigation:** The FDA's structured timeline and detailed feedback enabled Dozee to move through the complex regulatory landscape without costly detours.

- **Least-Burdensome Principle:** The agency accepted innovative testing and safety protocols proposed by the company, reducing unnecessary hurdles and shortening the review period.

- **Competitive Advantage:** FDA clearance opens a lucrative U.S. market that prizes innovation in patient monitoring. The approval validates Dozee's technology and operational rigour.

- **Foundation for Future Growth:** Successfully clearing one of the world's toughest regulatory bars positions Dozee for further expansion and continued innovation, reinforcing its vision of transforming global healthcare through advanced artificial intelligence.

A Blueprint for Protecting Vision Through Growth

Dozee's trajectory illustrates that strategic integrity can coexist with aggressive expansion. The founders never allowed the hunger for capital or quick scale to eclipse their original intent. Each funding round was paired with a clear milestone, each investor was vetted for philosophical fit, and every product enhancement was judged by its relevance to patient care rather than its press appeal. By holding fast to those guardrails, the company preserved authority over its own direction while still accessing the resources needed to compete on a global stage.

For founders navigating the same tightrope, the lesson is direct yet profound. Growth is not the enemy of vision, provided every decision is filtered through the lens of mission fidelity. Choose partners who amplify purpose, impose financial discipline that forces clarity, and treat regulatory rigour as a badge of credibility rather than a bureaucratic hurdle. Follow those rules with the same stubbornness that guided Dozee, and you can extend reach without diluting the spark that started it all.

Brewing a Brand Without Burning a Budget: The Blue Tokai Playbook

In an era where brand awareness often depends on headline-grabbing ad spends and turbo-charged expansion plans, **Blue Tokai Coffee Roasters** tells a quieter, slower story. Founded by **Matt Chitharanjan** and **Namrata Asthana**, the company shows how steady growth, disciplined fundraising, and unwavering focus on product integrity can build lasting resonance without surrendering equity or diluting the original idea.

Their narrative goes beyond coffee; it reframes how modern Indian consumers come to value taste, experience, and trust.

Phase 1: A Passion Brewed Through Precision

Blue Tokai did not emerge from a spreadsheet projection or a gap analysis. It began with a personal craving for better coffee.

Matt, raised in the United States, grew up on instant coffee and later shifted to Starbucks, more for convenience than flavour. A stint in San Francisco during the rise of the third-wave coffee movement opened his eyes. Coffee, he discovered, could reflect origin, roast profile, brewing method, and the meticulous care behind each cup.

When he moved to India in 2011 for a development project and later settled in Delhi, Matt and Namrata started roasting beans at home. At first it was a pastime, yet they approached it with an engineer's exactitude and an artist's sensibility. They sourced directly from estates, tracked roast curves, and documented every variable.

"We just wanted better coffee for ourselves. The fact that others wanted it too came later," Matt recalls.

That clarity—a product-first, process-driven mindset—became the brand's operating code. Each subsequent decision would trace back to that original mandate: deliver uncompromising quality and let growth follow at its own pace.

Phase 2: From Home Roaster to National Presence, All Without a Conventional Marketing Playbook

While many direct-to-consumer brands race ahead by pouring money into social ads and influencer tie-ups, Blue Tokai chose a quieter route.

"We have never spent more than two or three percent of revenue on marketing," Matt explains. "We put the rest into coffee and into the people who serve it."

Their growth engine turned out to be relentless consistency rather than paid reach. The system worked as follows:

- **Three central roasteries** guarded quality even as volumes climbed.
- **Company cafés** doubled as classrooms, inviting guests to taste origins, compare roast levels, and watch brewing in real-time.
- **Precision tools** such as automated grinders and calibrated tampers kept every pour-over or espresso within tight parameters, no matter the city.
- **An overstaffed support desk** treated service recovery as an act of hospitality; each resolved issue became an opportunity to deepen loyalty.

The result was a cup that felt personal in Delhi, Bengaluru, or any place in between. Blue Tokai didn't build a brand through storytelling; it became the story people told.

Phase 3: Strategic Capital Rather Than Capital as Strategy

Blue Tokai's fundraising mirrors its broader philosophy. Every rupee is purposeful, tied to milestones rather than momentum.

During the earliest months Matt and Namrata bootstrapped the venture, roasting beans in Namrata's parents' home and selling online. Growth eventually required outside money, but each round followed a clear plan rather than reflexive dilution.

- **Seed round in 2015** with Snow Leopard funded a move into a commercial facility and financed the first roastery café in Delhi.
- **Series A through Series C** arrived in stages, with bridge and internal tranches linked to measured outcomes such as new roasteries, loyalty programmes, and supply-chain upgrades.
- **Series C** led by Verlinvest focused on geographic expansion and on building deeper customer experience infrastructure.

"We are up to Series C and still break-even," Matt says. "We only raise what the next layer of responsible scale demands."

By avoiding the growth-at-all-costs mindset common in the café and quick service arena, Blue Tokai preserved operational discipline. Clarity consistently outranked speed.

Phase 4: Product Integrity as a Defensible Moat

As revenue shifted from a single roastery and e-commerce to a network where cafés now generate roughly eighty percent of sales, the central challenge became maintaining quality at volume. Rather than compromise, the team invested in systems that made scale a friend of flavour.

- **Central sourcing and roasting** maintained signature taste profiles across cities.
- **Training academies** nurtured talent, many recruits being first-time employees who progressed from barback to skilled barista.

- **Process automation**—precision grinders, calibrated tampers, water mineralisation tools—delivered uniform brews cup after cup.

"With size, you can actually push quality higher," Matt explains. "Equipment like colour sorters, advanced R and D labs, and structured training only made sense once we had the scale to use them fully."

Blue Tokai never accepted the idea that expansion must erode excellence. Instead, the company treated larger scale as leverage for deeper quality, rewriting the common storyline that pits growth against integrity.

Phase 5: Global Expansion Guided by Cultural Fit

In twenty-twenty-three Blue Tokai opened quietly in Japan and by twenty-twenty-five it poured its first coffees in Dubai. The choice of markets was anything but opportunistic. Each location mirrored a value that already lived at the heart of the brand.

Japan prizes craftsmanship, precision, and narrative, three qualities woven into every Blue Tokai roast profile and café ritual. Dubai hosts one of the largest and most prosperous Indian diasporas, an audience already familiar with the brand's origin story and eager for premium labels from home. Matt puts it simply, "Dubai feels like India's wealthiest city with even more spending power."

The expansions did more than lift topline revenue. They validated that a quiet, deliberate approach to quality resonates well beyond Indian metros.

Sustaining the Mission Through People and Practice

By twenty-twenty-five the company employs more than two thousand three hundred people and plans to add another fifteen hundred within the year. Service businesses of this size succeed only when communication is clear and values are lived daily. Matt's leadership playbook is straightforward.

- Cafés operate on five-day workweeks.
- After-hours messages are rare, personal time is respected.
- No tolerance exists for intimidation or raised voices.
- Training and internal mobility turn managers into executives.

He sums it up:

"Our baseline for culture is simple. Everyone should feel this is a place they want to be."

Culture is not treated as a perk. It functions as an operational advantage that keeps turnover low and customer experience high.

A Framework for Product-Led, Non-Dilutive Growth

Blue Tokai offers a counter narrative in India's direct-to-consumer landscape. While many brands chase viral campaigns, this company chooses craftsmanship. Where others scale through aggressive capital intake, it relies on robust systems and disciplined funding. Loud marketing gives way to quiet trust earned cup after cup.

For founders determined to grow without watering down their mission or product, the lesson is clear. Brand is not what you claim in an advertisement. Brand is what you serve, with unwavering consistency, to every customer who walks through the door. In a market full of noise, that consistency speaks loudest.

7.

The Pitfalls of Prioritising Storytelling and Fundraising

As the year 2022 drew to a close , the effects of the funding winter became unmistakable. The perils of chasing inflated valuations and securing fresh capital through compelling stories—rather than a well-grounded business model—were starkly exposed.

Tiny Owl: A Cautionary Tale of Image Over Substance

Amongst the startup stories that capture these hazards, **Tiny Owl** stands out as a notable example. Launched in 2014 as an Indian food-delivery app, it rocketed to notoriety with a catchy name, sleek branding, and an aggressive fundraising strategy. Yet in the span of just a couple of years, the venture collapsed as fast as it had ascended, offering an instructive reminder that building a brand narrative without solving real customer problems can be perilous.

The Rise: Storytelling That Sold

From the outset, Tiny Owl invested heavily in crafting a narrative that appealed to investors and the media. Its founding team described the venture as a cutting-edge tech solution poised to transform India's food-delivery market. Powered by a fresh, youthful spirit, the startup boasted an aspiration to dominate India's burgeoning urban sector.

This compelling story garnered major attention. In short order, Tiny Owl raised upwards of $20 million from heavyweight investors like Sequoia Capital and Matrix Partners—just a year into its existence. Surging capital, driven more by impressive pitches and lofty growth projections than by operational realities, made Tiny Owl a darling of the startup scene.

The problem? When a captivating narrative overshadows more pragmatic concerns, the gap between hype and the day-to-day realities of running a business can grow dangerously wide.

The Fall: Pursuing Growth While Overlooking the Essentials

Despite substantial funding, Tiny Owl soon revealed glaring internal and operational flaws. Management focused heavily on rapid city-by-city expansion—chasing market share above all else—rather than refining the product, responding to real customer needs, or fixing fundamental process gaps.

Growth-at-All-Costs Pitfalls

- **Operational Inefficiencies:** In rushing to enter new markets, Tiny Owl paid insufficient attention to local nuances. Weak restaurant partnerships, erratic delivery performance, and a sluggish response to customer complaints marred the user experience. Instead of resolving these core problems, the startup continued to burn through investor capital in pursuit of more users.

- **Workforce Mismanagement:** In 2015, Tiny Owl's reputation suffered a severe blow when it laid off nearly 300 employees in a disorganised and insensitive manner. The turmoil escalated when a co-founder was reportedly held hostage by angry staff in Pune, exposing a deeper cultural and leadership vacuum.

- **Neglecting Customer Value**
  Eager to fulfil investor expectations and maintain a compelling public profile, Tiny Owl lost sight of the very issue it claimed to solve: smooth food-delivery. Delayed orders, unreliable service, and inadequate customer support all suggested a widening gap between the brand's promise and actual user satisfaction.

The Role of Storytelling and Fundraising in Tiny Owl's Downfall

The core issue wasn't the act of storytelling itself—narratives can be powerful for unifying teams and attracting support. The real danger appears when the story overshadows actual value creation. Tiny Owl offers a stark illustration of this imbalance:

- **Investor Expectations vs. Operational Reality:** Tiny Owl wove a tale of boundless growth, driving its valuations and investor hopes to lofty heights. However, it neglected the fundamental operational flaws that could have validated these ambitions, eventually undermining its own credibility.
- **Burn Rate Over Value Creation:** Eager to maintain impressive growth numbers for investors, the startup spent aggressively. Yet little of that capital went toward building a solid infrastructure or resolving market-specific problems. Instead, it poured resources into marketing pushes and promotions to bolster its narrative.
- **Leadership Driven by Fundraising:** The founders spent more time appealing to investors than focusing on product quality or customer satisfaction. Over time, they became better known for securing funds than for building a user-focused offering.

Lessons for Entrepreneurs: Value Before Story

Tiny Owl's collapse highlights cautionary lessons for both founders and investors:

- **Solve a Real Problem First:** No matter how appealing the pitch, startups exist to address specific issues. If the core solution falters, a compelling story alone can't redeem it.

- **Keep Customers Front and Centre:** Satisfying end-user needs should outrank investor or marketing goals. Neglecting the customer experience is a recipe for long-term failure.

- **Emphasise Sustainable Growth Over Vanity Metrics:** Chasing glossy numbers without forging a solid, repeatable model is risky. Growth devoid of genuine value creation seldom endures.

- **Culture and People Are Critical:** The turmoil around Tiny Owl's layoffs revealed leadership and cultural deficiencies. A weak organisational foundation often unravels under pressure.

- **Use Fundraising as a Tool, Not a Trophy:** Securing capital is a step, not the destination. Measuring success by dollars raised—rather than by real impact—invites operational neglect and customer dissatisfaction.

While Tiny Owl raced through investor funds without fixing its operational core, **Porter**—founded at roughly the same time—chose a more disciplined path. Instead of pitching a high-stakes narrative, Porter focused on solving a tangible, overlooked challenge: the inefficiencies of intra-city logistics for small and medium businesses. Where Tiny Owl pursued hypergrowth before fully establishing its fundamentals, Porter concentrated on building trust with customers through a measured pace and careful attention to unit economics.

Even when Porter briefly fell prey to the allure of unchecked expansion after securing funding, it quickly reversed course— returning to its core emphasis on steady operational excellence rather than chasing fleeting trends. Tiny Owl ultimately collapsed under the weight of broken promises and internal chaos, whereas Porter's commitment to consistent value delivery, financial discipline, and customer-centric focus allowed it to weather challenges and grow sustainably.

Financial Discipline Over Storytelling: The Porter Playbook for Lasting Success

In India's frenetic startup scene—where compelling stories can secure capital faster than real businesses can form—**Porter** distinguishes itself by its quiet resolve, foundational rigour, and relentless attention to financial prudence. Instead of chasing lofty valuations through carefully spun narratives and funding theatrics, the Porter team chose a road that was more demanding, yet sustainable: building a real business set to grow and compound over the long haul.

Starting with a Problem, Not a Pitch

When **Uttam Digga**, along with co-founders **Pranav Goel** and **Vikas Choudhary**, launched Porter, they weren't motivated by the hype swirling around the Indian startup ecosystem in 2013–14. They began with systematic research into multiple sectors, seeking a concrete, overlooked problem. The outcome? An insight into **intra-city trucking inefficiencies**—an area where technology could bridge persistent gaps.

Their eureka moment occurred on an ordinary Mumbai bus ride, observing a landscape dotted with idle small trucks whose potential went largely untapped. The team pinpointed a twofold pain point:

- **Low Truck Utilisation**: Drivers regularly spent hours waiting for trips.

- **Trust Deficit**: Businesses at drop-off points hesitated to deal with unknown operators, often leaving trucks to return empty.

In effect, they saw a high fixed-cost, low-utilisation market in need of a tech-driven, trust-based solution. By concentrating on this real-world problem, Porter established the foundation for a durable business model rather than chasing ephemeral hype.

Building Slowly, Steadily—Not a "10x in a Year" Chase

From its start in 2014, **Porter** was never the type of startup that hit **10x or 15x growth** in a single year. While many peers chased rapid expansion, Porter opted for more modest yet reliable gains—100% to 150% annually, sustained over time. The founders recognised early on that their principal customers—small and medium enterprises—weren't quick to adopt new tools. Earning their trust required a consistent record of dependable service and tangible value.

The early days were anything but glamorous. In the first week after launch, Porter took in exactly zero orders, prompting serious soul-searching among the founders. However, their persistence eventually paid off. As more SMEs discovered the practical benefits Porter offered, growth began to accelerate.

Unlike startups that fixate on fundraising tied to ambitious future projections, Porter concentrated on building a solid operational core before actively pursuing larger sums of capital. Their story highlights that true sustainability emerges from sound business practices, not just compelling pitch decks.

The Temptations of Early Funding

Despite Porter's emphasis on fundamentals, even they felt the pull of easy money during 2015's euphoric fundraising climate. After landing their first investment within six months of launch—and quickly following up with a Series A from Sequoia—the team made a classic misstep: expanding in too many directions, too soon.

Flush with new capital, Porter branched out into intercity services, enterprise logistics, and ongoing support for SMEs, all at once. But by 2016, the funding winter had arrived. With capital drying up, Porter was forced to confront a hard truth: it had spread itself too thin. What followed was a pivotal reset:

- **Cutting Distractions**: Non-core segments such as intercity and enterprise logistics were shut down.
- **Refocusing on Core Strength**: The team doubled down on intra-city transportation for SMEs.
- **Tough Decisions**: Founders and key leaders took pay cuts, and transparency became central to the company's culture.

This lean phase, as Uttam recollected during his interview, became one of Porter's greatest advantages. It fostered a **discipline, focus, and sense of humility** that would guide them through future obstacles.

The Real Value of Financial Discipline: Survival and Strategic Focus

While many startups funneled money into vanity metrics, Porter stayed true to fundamentals like unit economics and city-level profitability. Lessons from the 2016 funding winter became embedded in Porter's culture. They sought capital only when they could show a clear return on investment, rather than using it to offset routine losses.

This prudence proved critical when COVID-19 shook global markets. Porter adapted rather than panicked:

- **Exiting Low-Margin Enterprise Deals**: Shedding segments that didn't align with profitability goals.
- **Pivoting to Relevant Services**: Introducing two-wheeler delivery and house shifting based on real-time demand and user feedback.
- **Reliance on Organic Loyalty**: Years of dependable service kept Porter's core user base strong despite external volatility.

Just as importantly, Porter's disciplined financial foundation allowed the company to optimise while competitors bled cash. Though difficult, the pandemic period gave Porter a chance to expand offerings and strengthen relationships with SMEs seeking reliable logistics.

Marketing: Grounded in Value, Not Flash

Instead of funneling massive budgets into high-profile ad campaigns, Porter chose a more pragmatic, results-driven marketing plan:

- **Organic Growth**: Roughly 85–90% of user acquisition still occurs naturally, propelled by satisfied customers who spread the word within their networks.
- **Local Network Effects**: Quality service in a specific region prompted SMEs to share recommendations with one another, slowly building market presence city-by-city.
- **On-the-Road Branding**: Trucks with the Porter logo offered cost-effective, hyper-local marketing, inspired by global examples like Lalamove.
- **Minimised Digital Spend**: Keeping CAC (customer acquisition cost) manageable by limiting expensive campaigns helped sustain long-term growth.

Through these steps, Porter consistently demonstrates that when marketing centres on reliability and user needs, growth follows at a sustainable pace.

Focusing on Purpose—Not Every Passing Trend

In a startup ecosystem where founders often chase the latest buzz—from dark stores to instant grocery—**Porter** has stayed true to its mission of supporting SMEs. Even when asked whether they'd venture into quick commerce, **Uttam** was clear:

> *"No, that's not our ethos. We exist to empower SMEs, not to become a B2C delivery company."*

This unwavering sense of direction contrasts sharply with many startups that pivot wherever the funding goes, rather than where tangible value can be created. Porter's steadfast dedication to its core audience—SMEs—serves as a powerful example of disciplined leadership.

The Compounder Mindset: How True Valuation Grows

Today, Porter operates in **22 cities**, aiming for **50**—not by raising billions to buy its way into growth, but by expanding methodically. Key elements of this approach include:

- **Measured City Expansion:** Each new market launch is carefully evaluated for profitability, even if it takes three to three-and-a-half years to see substantial returns.
- **ROI-Driven Decisions:** Porter only invests in new locales when the potential for a solid return is clear. Cities with over two million people, heavily populated with SMEs, fit the bill.
- **Stable, Real-World Valuation:** While many startups rely on hype to inflate numbers, Porter's worth rests on proven unit economics, steady expansion, and genuine customer trust.

The company's valuation has grown gradually and sustainably, reflecting years of careful scaling.

As Uttam observes,

> *"When a company grows, like an individual, it's hardships and discipline that shape its character. Businesses that weather adversity emerge tougher and more resilient."*

Porter's evolution stands as a guide for founders who aim to build lasting enterprises, not just short-lived success stories. Their story highlights that the loudest voice in the room doesn't always prevail; the one with focus, financial discipline, and persistence does. In a climate where the ability to raise funds can be mistaken for genuine achievement, Porter's journey is a reminder that long-term viability demands more doing than storytelling—and that strong fiscal fundamentals are the bedrock of any company built to endure.

Honey, Hold the Hype: Building the Long-Term Brand Behind Honey Twigs

Honey Twigs started with a problem: good honey was hard to use. It stuck to jars. Attracted ants. Spilled on countertops. And no one could carry it in their bag.

So Paras Fatnani and Jigar Mehta, who had met at University in London with backgrounds in marketing and a shared love of food, did something old-school—they spoke to 3,000 potential customers. Not to sell, but to listen. The verdict: people liked honey, but hated the mess, the uncertainty of quality, and the impracticality.

That insight built the company's foundation. Not branding. Not virality. A genuine need, tested and validated.

Their solution: a single-serve honey twig that made no-mess, on-the-go consumption possible. The first version leaked. So did the second. By the third round, they had a product they were proud of. One they'd use themselves—and only then, offer to the world.

Quality wasn't a tagline; it was an obsession. Every flavour was first tested in their own homes, across months. If their families didn't use it, they wouldn't sell it.

Distribution didn't begin with supermarkets. It started at farmers' markets, where a chance meeting led to a breakthrough deal with Café Coffee Day. No investor deck. No pitch. Just a buyer who saw real utility.

But building slowly came at a cost. For years, funding eluded them. Investors loved the product, but doubted the scale. So they bootstrapped. One angel investor came early. Another was their own honey supplier!

And then came ***Shark Tank India.***

By this point, Honey Twigs had weathered COVID (which wiped out 65% of their B2B business overnight), rebuilt their B2C channel, and started exporting to the U.S. They were ready. The national stage gave them what years of hustle hadn't—validation. The deal didn't close, but it didn't matter. Within 24 hours of the telecast, their phones didn't stop ringing. Customers wrote in. Orders exploded. The signal was loud and clear: the product worked.

Paras calls it their inflection point—not just in growth, but in confidence. It confirmed what they believed all along: when you build right, growth finds you.

Today, Honey Twigs remains grounded in the basics: customer feedback, patient iteration, financial restraint. Paras is clear-eyed about the two kinds of brands—the kind that scale on cash and fade when the money dries up, and the kind that become habits.

Because longevity isn't built on noise. It's built on quiet, deliberate choices—the kind that don't trend on Twitter, but do sit on kitchen shelves, day after day.

8.

The Strategic Importance of Diversification

IN A RAPIDLY changing world—one shaped by cutting-edge technologies and evolving consumer tastes—diversification has become a vital approach for businesses aiming to sustain and grow over the long haul. This chapter looks at how twenty top Indian companies have harnessed diversification not only to widen their market foothold but also to bolster their resilience against economic swings and ever-shifting market conditions.

The Essence of Diversification

At its core, diversification means extending a company's reach by incorporating new products, services, or markets into its existing mix. This method isn't just about chasing expansion; it's fundamentally a risk management strategy. By diversifying wisely, a business can safeguard its primary operations from sudden disruptions while capitalising on untapped opportunities for additional revenue and sustained growth.

The three case studies that follow—Wipro, Zomato, and Swiggy—offer practical illustrations of how strategic diversification can invigorate a company's long-term prospects.

From Oil to IT: Wipro's Reinvention

In the mid-20th century, **Wipro** was known chiefly for its consumer goods. Yet leadership sensed a shift on the horizon. As India opened up to global markets, newer opportunities began emerging beyond conventional manufacturing and goods.

The future, they realized, would hinge on industries propelled by knowledge and innovation rather than commodities alone.

Economic liberalisation in the 1980s and 1990s, coupled with the rapid ascent of computing, signalled a transformation in business priorities. Although Wipro's manufacturing interests remained steady, technology hinted at exponential growth. Instead of confining itself to its legacy sectors, the company made a daring move—harnessing its business acumen to pivot boldly into IT.

The Solution Was IT Services

Instead of tinkering around the edges, **Wipro** committed wholeheartedly to information technology, building new capabilities from the ground up around three foundational pillars:

- **Investing in Future-Ready Skills:** Without a technology background, Wipro fast-tracked its expertise by recruiting and training engineers and IT specialists. This shift let the company go beyond standard service provision, positioning itself as a technology adviser that could guide businesses through digital transformations.

- **Expanding Beyond India:** Recognising that IT services was a global market, Wipro pursued contracts in North America, Europe, and other international regions. Competing with major players like IBM and Accenture, Wipro's global outreach solidified its status as a leader in the international IT arena.

- **Adopting an Omnichannel Growth Strategy:** Borrowing from the approach that once fuelled its consumer goods success, Wipro broadened its IT offerings—covering software development, cloud solutions, cybersecurity, and business process outsourcing (BPO). By tailoring services to a diverse range of enterprise needs, it became a one-stop partner for organisations navigating digital transformation.

Wipro's journey was about more than just dipping a toe into a new sector—it was a calculated move to secure long-term relevance in an era of rapid change. While many legacy brands struggled to modernise, Wipro's courage to embrace a new direction has helped it evolve into one of India's leading IT services providers, demonstrating the significant rewards of strategic diversification and farsighted leadership.

How Swiggy and Zomato Reimagined Their Futures Through Strategic Diversification

India's startup scene thrives on reinvention, and few stories illustrate that spirit better than Swiggy and Zomato. Both began as restaurant delivery specialists and then, sensing shifting consumer habits and margin pressures, widened their horizons. Much like Wipro's leap from soaps to software, these consumer-tech giants used diversification to deepen relevance and build resilience in a market where competition is relentless.

Why Diversification Became Imperative

By the early twenty-twenties, Swiggy and Zomato had stitched together formidable delivery networks and powerful brands. Yet user expectations were racing ahead. Customers wanted instant solutions not just for meals but for groceries, documents, forgotten chargers, even the laundry bag left at a friend's place. At the same time platform economics were nudging both companies to find new revenue streams, pushing them to integrate vertically and broaden their service mix.

Rather than viewing these shifts as limitations, the two firms saw an invitation to evolve. Their ambition expanded from delivering food to orchestrating a larger ecosystem of convenience, logistics, and supply-chain control.

The Responses: Lifestyle Services and Deeper Infrastructure
Each company followed its own route, but the destination remained similar, namely sustained relevance through thoughtful diversification.

Swiggy: From Meals to Multi-Utility
Swiggy's evolution rests on two signature moves.
- **Swiggy Genie:** Realizing that its rider fleet could transport more than biryani boxes, Swiggy introduced a personal concierge. Need a laptop charger moved across town or a parcel dropped at the tailor? Genie converted ordinary errands into quick taps on an app, folding Swiggy into the everyday rhythm of urban life.
- **Swiggy Instamart:** Spotting the quick-commerce surge, Swiggy launched a grocery wing promising delivery in ten to thirty minutes. Using dark stores and a finely tuned supply-chain, Instamart shifted the brand from indulgence to daily necessity, making it the default choice for both planned stock-ups and last-minute cravings.

  These initiatives are more than side projects. Together they reposition Swiggy as a lifestyle utility, anchored in convenience and powered by logistics muscle.

Zomato: Shifting from Marketplace to Infrastructure Catalyst
Zomato decided to dig deeper into the supply-chain rather than branch outward. Its flagship move was **Zomato Hyperpure**, a business-to-business arm that sources top-grade ingredients, fresh produce, and kitchen essentials directly for restaurant partners. With Hyperpure, every tomato, grain of rice, and sanitizing agent is traceable to origin, tightening food safety and elevating consistency in restaurant kitchens, two priorities for today's discerning diners.

The programme reduces Zomato's dependence on outside suppliers, raises partner loyalty, and ultimately improves what reaches the consumer's plate by ensuring superior sourcing from day one.

Strategic Outcomes, Two Different Routes, One Goal

Swiggy widened its platform horizontally, adding consumer lifestyle services and micro-logistics. Zomato drilled vertically into supply chains. Although the tactics differ, the objectives align.

- **Omnichannel Discovery with Swiggy:** The app that once delivered dinner now handles groceries, parcels, and everyday errands, embedding itself deeper in user routines.
- **Full-Stack Reliability with Zomato:** The company matured from matchmaking orders to empowering restaurant success, lifting hygiene and food quality through direct supply control.

Reinvention as a Core Business Skill

Just as Wipro repurposed its problem-solving muscle from soaps to software, Swiggy and Zomato converted food tech know-how into broader ambitions. Diversification here is not random product addition; it is the foresight to spot adjacent needs, craft new service categories, and capture more of the value chain.

The payoff is higher relevance, stronger defences, and revenue lines that last beyond today's fashion. In a market that prizes speed and disruption, the winners are often those who redefine themselves before outside forces leave them no choice. Wipro moved from edible oils to operating systems, and Swiggy and Zomato now transform single deliveries into entire ecosystems. The lesson repeats: adapt early, expand wisely, lead confidently.

9.

The Habit Loop of Testing Market Fit

In his book **The Third Wave**, Alvin Toffler envisioned a future propelled by swift digital change. That future has arrived, and companies now operate in a climate where recalibrating product-market fit is routine. Agility—a readiness to pivot, an openness to constant reinvention—has become an essential trait for modern ventures. This section examines why reevaluating market fit is vital and how founders can adopt strategies that keep them flexible in shifting landscapes.

Understanding Market Fit:
Market fit describes how well a product aligns with a keen, ongoing demand. It isn't static. Technology advances and consumer tastes shift, compressing what once took decades into a handful of years. A platform, service, or product that felt perfectly matched to yesterday's needs might lag behind today's new standards.

Companies thrive when they look for emerging trends and signs that preferences are evolving. Spotting these shifts calls for consistent market research, a pulse on competition, and the courage to act quickly. In the digital realm, ignoring these signals can doom a great idea to irrelevance.

The Netflix Pivot
Picture 2006: Netflix existed, yet it was known for mailing DVDs straight to your home. It felt revolutionary, but it was also of its time. By 2024, streaming has reshaped how people watch movies

and shows, making the once-cherished DVD feel like a charming relic of yesteryear.

Netflix saw the horizon early and launched its streaming service in 2007. This wasn't a minor addition—this was a reimagining of how viewers found entertainment. Blockbuster, pinned to brick-and-mortar operations and physical rentals, found it difficult to let go of its original model. Netflix's choice to shift while Blockbuster hesitated highlights the power of anticipating change and acting on it. Netflix did more than adapt; it drove an entire sector toward a new normal.

Reed Hastings's approach, described in **No Rules Rules: Netflix and the Culture of Reinvention**, illustrates a culture that values bold moves. It shows how a company can lead when it's willing to question assumptions and remain open to continuous transformation.

Key Insights from No Rules Rules

- **First-Principle Thinking:** Netflix's pivot from DVDs to streaming grew out of a core question: how can we deliver entertainment in a more direct, sustainable way? By returning to basics—serving audiences as conveniently as possible—Netflix carved a path that supported growth on a global scale.
- **Investment in Technology:** Netflix bet early on Amazon Web Services (AWS) for cloud computing. That choice provided the flexibility to handle surges in user demand without building huge physical infrastructures. This shift toward scalable technology reinforced Netflix's ability to offer uninterrupted service, even as viewer numbers soared.
- **Localised Content Strategy:** When Netflix ventured into international territories, it recognised that every region has unique tastes. Funding local productions became a

linchpin in winning over audiences outside the United States. These investments expanded Netflix's subscriber base and underscored how an adaptable business model could accommodate cultural nuances on a global scale.

Market fit isn't one decision set in stone. Instead, it's an ongoing dynamic, continuously shaped by fresh discoveries, emerging tech, and the willingness to rethink a core strategy. Netflix made mistakes along the way, but it never stayed still.

Hastings's leadership style—highlighted by trust in talented teams, a focus on strong culture, and a commitment to continuous learning—demonstrates what it takes to guide a company through rapid expansion without losing sight of core objectives. The result is a case study in scaling while upholding quality and finding new ways to engage users.

Embracing Agility and Avoiding Rigidity

By revisiting market fit at regular intervals, businesses strengthen their resilience. A sense of rigidity forms when companies cling to old models or assume the market won't evolve. Netflix's evolution offers an alternative: pivot early when you sense bigger changes on the horizon, remain laser-focused on customer experience, and let cultural openness guide your strategic decisions.

More than anything, Netflix's rise shows that shifting gears isn't about mere survival. It's about seizing a transformative vision and steering an entire industry toward a future that seemed distant—until someone had the foresight to start building it.

When Netflix first embraced the shift toward streaming, it did more than follow a trend—it committed to a core competence: delivering on-demand content with consistent quality. That clarity of purpose formed the backbone of its global reach. Flexibility in processes, rather than rigid adherence to one playbook, allowed Netflix to navigate consumer behaviour shifts, market pivots, and new technologies. In an industry prone to rapid transformation, the only constant has been Netflix's refusal to stay static.

Lessons from the "Giants Who Fell"

Not every organisation transitions so smoothly. The digital era has propelled some companies into the spotlight and pressed others into obsolescence. Below, we explore three cautionary tales that illustrate what happens when a business fails to adapt in time.

1. **Blockbuster: Missing the Shift to Digital**
   - **The Cautionary Tale:** Blockbuster reigned over movie rentals for years, with thousands of locations and a familiar blue-and-yellow sign that hinted at weekend possibilities. Yet the convenience and breadth offered by on-demand streaming caught Blockbuster by surprise. The company clung to its retail-centric model, underestimating how swiftly digital platforms would evolve. By the time Blockbuster tried to pivot, it was outmaneuvered by Netflix and filed for bankruptcy in 2010.
   - **Key Takeaway:** Blockbuster's story highlights the need to recognise incoming trends and question legacy practices. Organisations that wait for the market to confirm changes often miss their chance to steer the direction themselves.

2. **Kodak: Inventing and Then Ignoring the Future**
   - **The Cautionary Tale:** Kodak symbolizes photography for many generations. The irony is that Kodak engineered the first digital camera in 1975, yet chose to protect its film business. While it hesitated, competitors seized the opportunity, with consumers quickly embracing digital cameras. That shift left Kodak's traditional model behind.

In 2012, Kodak filed for bankruptcy—proof that controlling today's market offers little guarantee about tomorrow.

- **Key Takeaway:** Innovation can become a liability if organisations fear cannibalising existing revenue streams. Growth often requires rethinking or even dismantling profitable lines of business to accommodate emerging technology.

3. **Borders: Overlooking the Digital Reading Revolution**
   - **The Cautionary Tale:** Borders once felt like a cornerstone of the book industry, packed with bestsellers and bustling coffee shops. As e-readers gained popularity, Borders chose to focus on brick-and-mortar sales rather than embracing digital distribution. Rival Barnes & Noble developed its own e-reader; Amazon made online ordering seamless. Borders arrived late to the party, tried to pivot when the market had already moved on, and closed all its stores by 2011.
   - **Key Takeaway:** In a climate where reading habits switched from paperbacks to digital screens, Borders lost momentum by ignoring early signals. Taking steps to embrace new channels, even if uncertain, can preserve long-term viability.

The collapse of these once-dominant giants points to a shared truth: legacy success rarely ensures future survival. In each case, corporate paralysis overshadowed the need for reinvention. The speed of digital transformation requires businesses to abandon complacency and treat every shift in consumer behaviour or technology as a prompt for evolution.

The Dangers of Rigidity

Companies like Kodak and Blockbuster illustrate how rigid strategies become liabilities in a changing world. A market that once rewarded a certain formula may no longer sustain it. Rigid thinking stifles experimentation, locking teams into outdated patterns even as customers, competitors, and technologies move ahead.

Strategies for Maintaining Market Fit

1. **Continuous Market Analysis**
   - **Stay Attuned**: Watch trends, observe competitive manoeuvres, and survey customer feedback regularly.
   - **Identify Emerging Gaps**: Be quick to recognise opportunities—whether for new products or updated positioning.

2. **Fostering a Culture of Innovation**
   - **Encourage Experimentation**: Welcome ideas from all levels. Pilot new features or processes, even when they challenge current methods.
   - **Embrace Failure**: Teams that feel safe failing explore possibilities more freely, often producing transformative solutions.

3. **Leveraging Data and Technology**
   - **Informed Insights**: Use analytics to pinpoint consumer preferences, shipping bottlenecks, or evolving patterns in usage.
   - **Guided Strategy**: Align development cycles, marketing strategies, and new feature rollouts with data-driven evidence.

4. **Agile Methodologies**
   - **Cross-functional collaboration**: Bring diverse teams together to tackle projects in short sprints.
   - **Rapid Iterations**: Release manageable updates, gather feedback quickly, and refine before challenges become unmanageable.

5. **Strategic Partnerships and Collaborations**
   - **Expand Horizons**: Partner with startups for leading-edge tech or team up with complementary brands for co-branded initiatives.
   - **Shared Knowledge**: Collaborations open doors to new customer segments and innovative solutions.

In a business climate evolving at digital speed, the battle isn't simply about having the best current product. True sustainability resides in a willingness to adapt—constantly recalibrating, drawing on fresh insights, and anticipating trends before they reshape the market. These actions guard against the subtle drift into obsolescence. Agility, more than any single advantage, stands as the pillar supporting future growth and enduring relevance.

10.

The Power of Invisible Work: Building Foundations That Scale

STARTUPS THRIVE ON the visible highs—funding headlines, hockey-stick user charts, and splashy product launches. Yet the forces that sustain long-term success often remain out of sight. They include tight operations, documented processes, a resilient culture, and customer support that never misses a beat. In the race to scale these quieter disciplines are frequently postponed, only to resurface when momentum collapses under its own weight. Strong roots support tall trees, and companies with well-tended back ends can rise without stumbling once real volume arrives.

- **Foundational Work**
- **Sales Process**
- **Culture**
- **Tools**

What You Fix Today Pays Tomorrow
Lessons from the Solutions Infini Acquisition

Ashish and Aniketh felt prepared when acquisition talks heated up. They had launched Solutions Infini straight out of college, hustled through freelance work, recruited a committed team, and built respectable revenue. However, once Ubiquity's due-diligence team opened its files, every neglected detail from the past resurfaced.

The first shock was documentation, or the spaces in it. Years devoted to winning clients and putting out daily fires had left the back office in disarray. Profit by customer? No ledger. Gross-margin history? Missing. Segment contribution? Uncalculated. Ashish later reflected they had built the product but youthful naiveite' did not prioritise building the "company health record" that investors consider essential from day one.

Process gaps followed close behind. As a bootstrapped outfit they had explored services from software development to web hosting before settling on cloud communications. Traces of those early experiments still cluttered the operation. Business lines overlapped and workflows twisted into tangles that now required painful explanation. What once looked like youthful versatility now appeared as inefficiency under the lens of an international acquirer.

And then came the collections nightmare. Aniketh recalled that during acquisition talks they still had customer invoices outstanding for years, with no formal follow-up system in place. That lapse nearly torpedoed the deal. He explained, "If you cannot control receivables, what value does your revenue figure really carry?"

Control over the core product was another gap. For several years the messaging service ran on a reseller arrangement that relied on outside vendors. Only after Ashish completed a marathon coding sprint did they own a proprietary platform. Those lost years showed up clearly in weaker margins and softer customer loyalty, a vulnerability that Ubiquity's analysts noted.

The push for cross-border growth revealed the biggest contrast. Kaleyra was already scaling globally, while Solutions Infini discovered that international compliance demands, regulatory filings, and structural complexities differed vastly from the domestic environment.

Facing these shortcomings became a turning point. Guided by a banker-adviser who imposed operating discipline, they cleaned up systems and renegotiated on the promise of future value creation. The company later listed on the NYSE and eventually was acquired by Tata Communications.

In 2022 Ashish and Aniketh began their next venture, FYNO. This time every process was intentional: thorough documentation, disciplined collections, and a clear lens on profitability at the customer level. As second-time founders they aimed not just for speed but for foresight and purpose.

From their conversation we distilled five practices to follow and five pitfalls to avoid.

Five Things to Do

1. Maintain detailed documentation from day one. Investors will ask for profitability by customer, margin history, and growth trends.
2. Focus early on the core business. Their pivot to pure messaging put them on the path to profit.
3. Build proprietary platforms instead of reselling other products. Ownership brings control and higher valuation.
4. Systematize collections and customer contracts. Poor receivables management almost derailed their acquisition.
5. Prepare for global requirements early. If international expansion is even a distant goal, align compliance and documentation now.

Five Things to Avoid

1. Do not postpone processes because you feel too small. Skipping structure costs more later.
2. Do not stay scattered across multiple lines once you know what works. Prolonged dabbling slows momentum.
3. Do not ignore receivables. Outstanding payments nearly broke the Solutions Infini deal.
4. Do not rely on resellers for critical offerings. Building your own product is time intensive; begin sooner.
5. Do not assume global markets mirror domestic ones. International regulations and standards raise the bar.

SALES

Building Resilience, Relationships, and Results

When the economy stalls, one function keeps moving steadily forward, namely sales. Consumer demand rises and falls with sentiment, yet business to business transactions often hinge on necessity. Companies still need software, infrastructure, and services that lift efficiency, trim expenses, and protect output. During downturns decision makers actively search for solutions that promise continuity and savings, which gives B2B sales unusual stamina through business cycles.

Enterprise deals run on multi-year contracts rather than single purchases. The relationships are strategic, decisions deliberate, and outcomes long-term. For a startup that wants to grow its enterprise footprint, hiring a few account executives is not enough. A resilient sales engine rests on seven pillars: market positioning, lead generation, sales narratives, internal incentives, onboarding, conversion metrics, and negotiation skills.

1. **Find Your Place on the Spectrum**

   The Indian B2B landscape is vast and varied. Opportunity exists for every startup that positions itself wisely. Consider the automotive market. Porsche, Kia, and MG entered India when analysts claimed the field was full. Porsche focused on performance luxury, Kia on value with design flair, and MG on technology driven comfort. Each brand chose a distinct spectrum slot.

   For B2B, a spectrum slot could mean serving mid-size firms instead of Fortune-five-hundred giants or offering modular pricing instead of long lock-ins. Many founders aim too broadly too soon. The smarter route is a narrow beachhead backed by deep customer insight. Your spot on the spectrum is where your product resolves a problem that is important, urgent, and valuable for a specific buyer group.

2. **Solving the Perennial Lead Problem**

In enterprise sales the hardest part is not persuasion, it is discovery. Quality leads require both art and science. Practical steps include:

- **BANT**, qualifying prospects for budget, authority, need, and timing
- **Lead scoring**, ranking contacts by engagement and fit with the ideal customer profile
- **Buyer personas**, crafting semi-fictional archetypes to tailor outreach
- **Pre-call research**, arming representatives with context so conversations start with insight

Pair these methods with a steady demand engine built on content marketing, strategic partnerships, outbound campaigns, and referrals. Only then will consistent quality reach the top of the funnel.

Leads mark the beginning, not the finish. Next comes close attention to funnel metrics.

3. **Understanding Your Sales Funnel and Metrics**

An efficient funnel does more than park leads; it extracts maximum return on every sales effort.

- **Top of funnel (TOFU)**: impressions, content engagement, inbound visits
- **Middle of funnel (MOFU)**: qualified leads, demo bookings, discovery calls
- **Bottom of funnel (BOFU)**: proposals, negotiations, closed deals

Key conversion checkpoints
- Lead to MQL (Marketing Qualified Lead)
- MQL to SQL (Sales Qualified Lead)
- SQL to demo rate
- Demo to proposal rate
- Proposal to close rate

Watching and improving each ratio lets sales managers diagnose issues quickly. For example, if the proposal to close figure sits below twenty percent, the trouble likely lies in pricing, positioning, or stakeholder alignment rather than lead volume. Weekly funnel reviews tied to revenue forecasts ensure the team is not just busy but truly moving forward.

4. **Mastering the Pitch with Listicles**

In a world short on attention, complexity kills conversion. Many of today's best sales decks borrow a tactic from content marketing: the listicle. Breaking the pitch into five or seven concise points adds order and cognitive ease, useful in hybrid calls and executive briefings alike.

- **Clarity**: simplifies technical detail
- **Recall**: leaders remember a few strong points, not a monologue
- **Shareability**: easy for champions to forward or repeat internally
- **Strategic flow**: points can be arranged by impact, cost, or speed
- **Decision support**: guides buyers through evaluation with clear logic

Pairing sharp lists with solid insights and clean visuals turns scepticism into agreement.

5. **Incentives Drive Behaviour**

A flawless sales playbook still fails if compensation pulls reps in the wrong direction. Enterprise deals are lengthy, intricate, and team driven, yet many startups bolt on retail-style, quick-win commission plans. Build structures that match the reality of complex cycles.

Designing Smarter Incentives

- **Reward learning and progression**, paying for milestones such as qualified meetings, stakeholder maps, and proposals, not only closed deals.

- **Use team bonuses**, pooling rewards across sales, product, and customer success for key accounts.
- **Tie payouts to long-term value**, giving credit for renewals and expansions so reps avoid overpromising.
- **Add accelerators for strategic accounts**, offering richer commissions when landmark clients convert.

Incentives act as culture in disguise. Set them correctly and the right mindset follows.

6. **Make Onboarding Part of the Sales Cycle**

Onboarding is the final stage of the funnel and the first step toward retention. Poor handovers erode trust, while smooth launches turn users into champions.

Why Onboarding Matters

- Early impressions shape perceived product quality.
- Quick value reduces churn.
- Fast adoption shortens time to value.
- Clarity builds confidence and trust.
- Successful users generate referrals and renewals.

A well trained customer becomes your best internal advocate.

7. **Negotiation, Where Strategy Meets Psychology**

Negotiation does not start at contract stage; it begins the moment discovery ends.

Core Principles

- **Anchor first**, leading with your proposal and value frame.
- **Identify all stakeholders**, knowing who signs and who blocks.
- **Trade, do not give**, exchanging every concession for equal value.
- **Be ready to walk**, confidence often outweighs price.
- **Create urgency by value**, not artificial scarcity.

Strong negotiators align departments, eliminate friction, and leave a model others can repeat.

8. **Avoiding Invisible Blockers**
    Sales momentum usually dies from hidden snags, not product flaws.
    Common Pitfalls
    - Overreliance on tools, forgetting that trust closes deals.
    - Confirmation bias in targeting and optimism bias in forecasting.
    - Generational gaps, where leadership wants reports and junior teams live in Slack.
    - Siloed feedback, failing to review and refine narratives regularly.

    Sales is applied behavioural psychology. The more human the approach, the more scalable the engine.

In conclusion, sales is not pure hustle; it is an architecture of trust. Built correctly, it weathers recessions, survives cycles, and multiplies value. Measure each stage, reward lasting success, treat onboarding as a core function, and remember that closing a deal is only the beginning of the customer's transformation.

HR and Culture
Why HR Matters From Day One

Startup momentum often centres on product features, growth hacks, and investment milestones. Yet behind every high-performing team and durable business model sits a factor that many founders recognise only after trouble starts, culture. Not culture as in foosball tables and Friday lunches, but a shared operating code that dictates how people behave, decide, and persevere on the hardest days.

Culture, the Startup's Invisible Engine

Picture culture as the unseen motor beneath company operations. When robust, it drives teams through pivots and uncertainty. When weak, it erodes morale, accountability, and results. Early culture flows from founders, from what they reward, what they shrug off, and what they challenge in real-time. A founder's reaction to missed targets, ethical grey zones, and rough quarters becomes part of collective memory.

A cautionary pattern, during India's first funding boom many startups scaled headcount without screening for culture fit and soon wrestled with fragmented teams and clashing agendas. High churn, politics, and execution gaps often traced back to cultural missteps rather than flawed strategy.

Laying the Foundation, The Five Pillars of High Performance Culture
Clarity of Purpose

Vision statements are not enough. Every hire must link personal work to a larger mission. Knowing not only what they build but why it matters fuels ownership when roles blur and resources thin.

Open Communication

In rapid growth, silos can be fatal. Founders must live radical transparency, sharing wins, setbacks, financial realities, and customer feedback. Weekly town halls or monthly ask me anything sessions flatten hierarchy and build trust.

Bias for Action, Tolerance for Failure

Thriving cultures make space for experiments. Teams are urged to test ideas, fail quickly, and share lessons. Leaders celebrate sincere missteps and forbid blame games, avoiding the risk averse mindset that smothers innovation.

Respect and Inclusivity

Variation in thought and background is a strategic asset. From day one founders must enforce zero tolerance for bias. Provide clear feedback channels, resolve grievances promptly, and welcome dissent rather than silence it.

Recognition and Growth

Startups demand much from employees, so reward effort and map career paths. Public praise, learning budgets, and regular development check-ins keep motivation high through long stretches of grind.

HR Practices Are Not Just for Corporates

For founders, HR is not a "big company problem." The best startups treat HR as a strategic lever, not a compliance checkbox. Here are proven practices to build early: Treat HR as a strategic lever, not a paperwork chore.

Intentional hiring

Hire slowly and release quickly when misalignment appears. Screen for cultural fit with the same rigour used for skills. Use structured interviews and reference checks that probe values, not only achievements.

Onboarding with purpose

First impressions endure. Craft an onboarding journey that immerses each new hire in the company story and working style. Do more than product demos and forms.

Continuous feedback loops

Replace the yearly appraisal with monthly one-on-ones, pulse surveys, and skip-level meetings. Early conversations stop small issues from becoming cultural cracks.

Compensation and incentives

Share pay, equity, and bonus logic openly. Tie rewards to personal output and team results so collaboration wins over silo goals.

Well-being and flexibility

Hustle matters, but burnout helps no one. Encourage sane work hours, real-time off, and mental health resources. Energised founders create energised teams.

In Short: Walk the Talk

Founders set the tempo. If you want honesty, model it in your weekly reviews. Don't sugarcoat bad news. Say things like *"We missed our numbers, and here's why I think it happened. What do you think?"* Openness turns feedback into routine, not exception.

If work–life balance is promised, model it. Take a break, share the photo, avoid late-night emails. Your example grants others permission to recharge.

Language shapes behaviour. When leaders talk only about tickets and targets, teams optimise for them. Speak equally about impact, empathy, and delight, and dashboards will start to reflect those aims.

Inclusivity thrives in tone, not policy alone. Do junior engineers feel safe asking questions? Does customer support have a say in product calls? Notice who gets interrupted and correct it.

Even volume carries meaning. A loud office where misses earn public scolding builds fear, not urgency. A calm space where leaders coach builds trust and speed.

The best cultures are not loud, they're clear.

When founders value how the work gets done as much as the product itself, they encourage teams that solve problems quickly, cooperate naturally, and stay longer. A fancy title like Chief Culture Officer is optional; intention, reflection, and steady follow-through are not.

Narayan R T, former People Partner at Accel, puts it plainly:

"Good culture lowers attrition and lifts engagement, which shows up in both the bottom line and company valuation."

While the headcount climbs, pause every few months and ask:

- Is our culture still serving us?
- What has changed since we were ten people around one table?
- Do new hires feel the same ownership and purpose that early colleagues enjoyed?

Remember, culture never sits still. Each hire, policy tweak, and hallway anecdote nudges it in a new direction.

TOOLS

Equipping the Zero-to-X Journey: India-Focused Picks for Founders

In the earliest chapters of a startup, founders juggle many roles. Progress in this zero-to-X phase relies on tools that cut busywork, surface data, and keep everyone aligned. Below is a snapshot of widely used options across the Indian ecosystem.

1. **Product and Engineering**

   Great intuition sparks ideas, but quick feedback fuels growth.

   - **Figma** remains the standard for collaborative design.
   - **GitHub** anchors version control, while **Jira** and **Zoho Sprints** run agile backlogs.
   - For user analytics, many teams turn to **CleverTap** or **MoEngage**, with **Google Analytics** still a staple.
   - On the cloud side, **AWS Activate** grants credits to young Indian startups; **Microsoft Azure** is a close second.

2. **Sales and CRM**

   Founders often serve as the first sales reps, so structure matters.

   - **HubSpot CRM** offers a popular free tier that tracks emails and deals.
   - **LinkedIn Sales Navigator** remains essential for B2B outreach.
   - **LeadSquared** automates follow-ups, and **Freshsales** by Freshworks links sales, marketing, and support.
   - **Google Calendar** paired with **Zoom** keeps demo scheduling smooth and professional.

3. **Marketing: Stretch Budgets, Scale Discovery**

   Cost efficiency is vital for early-stage promotion.

   - **Performance channels**: Google Ads and Meta Ads still pull the largest reach, while **WebEngage** and **CleverTap** help teams retain and re-engage users.

- **Creative tools**: Canva remains the quick design favorite, and **Zoho Social** schedules posts across Indian networks.
- **SEO stack**: Google Search Console, Ubersuggest with India-friendly pricing, and Ahrefs (popular in later stages) surface high-intent keywords.
- **List building**: Mailchimp and Zoho Campaigns get newsletters out quickly.
- **Authority building**: YouTube delivers the best long-form return on investment for founders who want organic discovery.

4. **Customer Success and Support: Turn Retention into Growth**

   Winning companies keep users, not just acquire them.
   - **Service desks**: Freshdesk and Zoho Desk scale customer support at local price points.
   - **Onboarding aids**: Loom for video walkthroughs and WhatsApp Business for direct updates.
   - **Feedback loops**: Typeform, Google Forms, and SurveyMonkey gather sentiment, while FullStory or Smartlook reveal user journeys.
   - **Primary channel in smaller cities**: WhatsApp remains the go-to touchpoint.

5. **Finance and Operations: Discipline from the Start**

   Financial hygiene cannot wait for revenue.
   - **Accounting**: Zoho Books, TallyPrime, and QuickBooks India handle ledgers and invoices.
   - **Payroll and compliance**: GreytHR, Keka, and RazorpayX Payroll automate salaries and filings.
   - **Payments**: Razorpay and Cashfree integrate with sites and apps, while Open (the startup neobank) streamlines banking dashboards.

- **Reporting**: Google Sheets still underpins projections, KPI scorecards, and investor updates.

6. **Hiring and Team Collaboration: Assemble the Right People**

Talent sets the pace of growth.

- **Recruitment**: LinkedIn Recruiter heads founder-led searches, with AngelList India, Instahyre, and Naukri.com filling tech and business roles.
- **Productivity suites**: Google Workspace and Microsoft 365 lead adoption.
- **Communication**: Slack keeps teams in sync, and Notion or Zoho Projects organise docs, onboarding, and internal wikis.

Indian startups run lean, so choose tools that add clarity, not clutter. Build your stack in line with stage and bandwidth, letting each platform serve a clear purpose on the zero-to-X journey

CONCLUSION

WHEN I BEGAN writing *Venture Theory* in August 2023, it quickly dawned on me that I wasn't just chronicling startup stories—I was chronicling patterns. Across boardrooms and dinner tables, from too many coffee-laced conversations to Zoom calls that stretched into the night, I listened to founders who had faced down chaos, and, in some cases, redefined entire categories.

Interestingly, I had first come across the term "Venture Theory" in a research paper back in 2019. It immediately struck a chord. Since then, I've used it as a mental model in enterprise sales training sessions and in coaching founders—especially to explain how even seemingly small decisions carry disproportionate weight in influencing long-term outcomes. It gave language to what I was already seeing play out: that behind every resilient outcome, was a series of mindful, compounding choices.

While I got great insights into stories of stellar success and resilience, I also came across stories and lessons from those who stumbled—not for lack of ambition, but often because they couldn't translate intent into execution, or pace into progress.

And that is what *Venture Theory* sets out to solve. At its core, this book is a blueprint for reducing the failure rate of startups.

Each of the ten chapters is less a rigid blueprint and more a toolkit of sharp insights—helping founders pause, rethink, and recalibrate how they're building.

Together, they bring *Venture Theory* to life as a daily discipline: the quiet, consistent habit of making better decisions, one thoughtful move at a time.

This isn't a 100-slide strategy deck. It's a way of thinking—and building—with intent.

We spotlighted how **iterative product development** can break through perfection paralysis. Why **customer acquisition** isn't a performance marketing playbook, but a journey of trust. We saw how **premature scaling** can hollow out momentum, and why storytelling without substance can raise money but not loyalty. We explored the brand-building journeys of real founders—those who chose consistency over virality, and emotional equity over mere impressions.

We discussed the **non-dilution challenge**, not as a fundraising tactic, but as a reminder that vision is a long game. We examined **financial discipline**, not to glorify frugality, but to show how misaligned metrics can unravel promising ideas. We studied **diversification**, not as a scale strategy, but as a survival instinct. We underlined the importance of **testing for market fit**—not once, but habitually. And perhaps most importantly, we highlighted the **invisible work**—processes, infrastructure, team rituals—that often determine whether a startup is built to last.

The Ultimate Ambition of Venture Theory?

It is to help the next generation of founders **fail better, or not fail at all.**

According to industry data, more than 90% of startups still don't make it past Series A. But that's not because the ideas were bad—it's because the systems, decisions, and disciplines didn't align in time. Our hope is that *Venture Theory* serves as a companion for every founder navigating those early, uncertain years. Not a guru, not a guarantee—but a guide.

I didn't want to write a book that's shelved once read. I wanted to build a reference manual you can return to—when growth stalls, when teams splinter, or when the shine of a launch wears off and the real work begins. Like a textbook where you've made your own notes in the margins, underlined sentences and dog-eared important pages.

Because in the end, *Venture Theory* is not just a book.

It is the voice of a guide/strategic advisor/trusted mentor.

That the difference between the ones that survived and the ones that didn't wasn't luck, or funding, or timing. It was in the **micro-decisions made daily**, the systems embedded quietly, and the patience to build better, not faster.

And if this book can help more founders embrace that truth, then perhaps, we can tip the scales.

And the 21 months of work that went into writing this book – was well spent.

Towards fewer failures.

And many more stories worth telling.

Thank you for reading.
Now go build something great!

- Sowmya

DEDICATION

To best tribe a girl can ask for—
My forever-first responders to every spiral, emergency, and shields to that ability of mine to magnificently overthink.
You believed I could write this book on days I couldn't remember why I started.
You cheered, edited, interrogated, intervened, distracted, and most importantly—stayed.
And some of you just showed up with food, advice, strong coffee, and perspective that held more clarity than my muddled brain caught up in writing fog held at certain points.
Thank you for being the compass when I lost direction, and the proof that I never had to do this alone.

To my family—
Thank you for tolerating the ghost version of me, the one that vanished into headphones and deadlines, resurfacing at home only twice in 2025 both times for food.
I know I've missed Sunday lunches. I promise to come home more often.

To the founders and investors who let me in—
Thank you for your courage in sharing what doesn't make it to pitch decks or PR campaigns.
You trusted me with the raw footage behind the highlights: the sleepless nights, quiet wins, scrapped ideas, and shaky first steps.
This book exists because of your candour, your vulnerability, and your relentless belief that it's worth building something better.

To Rohit—
You somehow read my mind and then out-designed it.
The cover, the website, the magic you added—they're all proof that beauty can emerge from chaos (and late-night WhatsApp briefs).

To Sayali—
You lifted the entire marketing campaign like it was light as air and ran with it like it was fire.
I don't know how you did it, but I know I'm grateful you did. This launch has your fingerprints all over it—in the best possible way.

And finally,

To Shonu and Siddu—
A teenager and a not-so-little boy in a hurry to be one later this year.
This book is for you.
For the kind of world I hope you'll create. One where ideas matter, kindness scales, and your stories shape more than just headlines.